How to Thrive in Associate Staff Ministry

KEVIN E. LAWSON
FOREWORD BY LOVETT WEEMS, JR.

AN ALBAN INSTITUTE PUBLICATION

Copyright © 2000 by the Alban Institute. All rights reserved.

This material may not be photocopied or reproduced in any way without written permission.

Library of Congress Card Number 99-69582
ISBN 1-56699-227-3

08   07   06   05   04   WP   3   4   5   6   7   8   9   10   11   12

CONTENTS

FOREWORD

One long-standing gap in congregational leadership literature has been research on the role of associate pastors and other professional staff members. Much of the writing on multiple-staff ministry has been from the perspective of the senior pastor. Kevin Lawson has made a major contribution in addressing the distinctive needs, circumstances, and opportunities of staff ministry. This study comes at an opportune time, as many churches are expanding staffs, particularly by adding lay professional staff members.

In *How to Thrive in Associate Staff Ministry*, Lawson combines in a masterful way his scholarly research skills with his experience as a minister of Christian education in local churches of three denominations. His research methods are solid, and his illustrations from his own experience and that of the dozens of local-church staff members he studied are authentic and appropriate.

There is a renewed appreciation today in the church for the importance of "practices" in one's growth in Christian discipleship. Likewise, in the business world much emphasis is given to the study of "best practices" within particular industries as a way to learn from the example of others in order to improve. In essence, Lawson is drawing from both of these important understandings in his approach to studying staff ministry.

Lawson deals with the problems of staff ministry, but problems are not the beginning point. This book is about ministry enhancement, not problem-solving. His study focuses on long-serving staff ministers who are thriving in such ministry. His purpose is to identify those practices that promote longevity, satisfaction, and personal well-being. The corollary goal is to find ways that staff ministers, as well as their supervising pastors and lay committees, can incorporate these practices to support the vitality of congregational ministry and mission.

The positive and constructive stance of this book makes it a valuable resource. Often enormous energy is misspent on matters of standing and prerogative, since staff members normally suffer from lower status, salary, influence, and job security. Lawson correctly frames the issues around one's calling to ministry.

In Luke 22:24 (NRSV), a dispute arises among the disciples as to "which one of them was to be regarded as the greatest." This is the wrong question, but one that is asked all too often within church staffs. Authority in the Bible has to do with a responsibility, not a privilege. Christian authority is not about our status in relationship to others but about God's will for each of us and how faithful we are in fulfilling God's call.

Theologian Letty Russell speaks of the "power of purpose" in contrast to the "power of position." It is the church's mission and the vision for a particular congregation that must guide all ministries among the ordained, other staff, and laity. Christian authority is always about the fulfillment of God's vision. When leaders take their eyes off the larger vision, and focus instead on where they stand in relationship to others in a hierarchy, then energy is misdirected and leadership ceases to be faithful.

Lawson points church staffs to specific questions and practices that can move the conversation away from "who is to be regarded as greatest among us." Some better questions for leaders and congregations may be:

- What is your particular calling from God? (calling).
- Do you have what you need to fulfill your calling? (support).
- Are you being faithful in fulfilling your calling? (accountability).

These questions put the focus not on one's status in relationship to others, but on one's relationship to God's vision for oneself.

In the marvelous wisdom of God, all of God's servants may then come to experience power not as a fixed sum that must be carefully appropriated. Instead, power will become an infinitely expandable sum, as all become strong for their particular callings and, at the same time, make sure that all other colleagues are strong for their own callings. We also come to see that all of us have authority in different ways based on the unique callings that God, the church, and our context place upon us.

LOVETT H. WEEMS, JR.
President, Saint Paul School of Theology
Kansas City, Missouri

PREFACE

It is with great concern, excitement, and deep appreciation that I offer this book to those who serve as associate staff members. I am concerned because I understand the range of issues and stresses that can turn ministry into a frustrating experience. I have felt some of these stresses, and I know many people who, having started in vocational ministry as associate staff members, left it altogether within a few years. I am excited because of all that I have learned over the past few years from long-term associate staff members about what helps them thrive in their ministries. They hold out hope to all of us that thriving is possible, and they show us how we can move toward it. I also deeply appreciate all the time, effort, and support that others have invested in helping with the successful completion of this research project and the writing of this book.

This project grows out of the support of several groups in a major research effort. The Louisville Institute provided major funding for the "Thriving in Associate Staff Ministry" research project. In addition, the North American Professors of Christian Education (NAPCE) and Biola University contributed grants to make the research possible. Many professional organizations cooperated in the focus-group phase of the study, including the Professional Association of Christian Educators (PACE), Youth Specialties, the International Network of Children's Pastors (INCP), MusiCalifornia, Hume Lake Conference Center, the Dallas (Texas) Southern Baptist Church Association, and many friends in ministry in Canada and southern California. In addition, I deeply appreciate the cooperation and assistance of leaders in many denominational offices who provided assistance with the survey portion of the study.

Many people assisted with data analysis, making my task easier. Special thanks to Christy Morr and Doris Anderson, who typed transcripts of the focus-group sessions; Dave Keehn and Brent Hinsley, who helped lead and analyze the youth-pastor focus groups; Shelly Cunningham, who helped lead the focus groups of women associate staff members; the students at Canadian Theological Seminary, who helped me process much of the focus-group data in a course I taught as guest faculty; my wife, Patty, who did data input from the surveys; and my students and colleagues at Talbot School of Theology, Biola University, who encouraged me, provided time for research and writing, and continued to be patient with me as I worked through this project. Finally, I express my appreciation to my children, Laura, Nathan, and Sarah, who patiently put up with all the trips I took over the two years I have worked on this effort.

May this book assist and encourage those who want to serve, and those who now serve, in associate staff positions in God's church.

Really Thriving vs. Barely Surviving

This book was written to help church workers break out of a survival mode in ministry and reach the point of thriving as associate staff members. But what does it mean to thrive in associate staff ministry and not merely survive? Because the boundary between these two experiences can be a little fuzzy, it may be helpful to begin by looking at each experience in its extreme.

Probably we each have our own intuitive sense of what it means to thrive in our work. If we had to describe it, we might speak of having a sense of personal well-being, contentment, and satisfaction in our ministry. We might even talk about finding joy and fulfillment in our work. Our involvement in this ministry, though difficult at times, is energizing, not draining. This sense of thriving is not necessarily due to the ministry's going smoothly, because that state of affairs can fluctuate. The ability to thrive is based not on the absence of stress or frustrating situations but on the ability to continue to work in the midst of them, not growing excessively discouraged or drained by them.

In contrast, if we had to describe the experience of barely surviving, we might complain of feeling drained by work responsibilities and feeling that life is stressful and out of balance. Dissatisfaction and a lack of contentment would mark how we viewed our ministry. We would gain little sense of fulfillment from our ministry, even when things were going smoothly. The work might get done, and we might cope with the stresses, but our work would be only a matter of survival and going through the motions.

In the survey responses of more than 400 long-term associate staff members in 14 denominations in the United States and Canada, the difference between the extremes of really thriving and barely surviving was described this way:

A person who is really thriving: *This is a good ministry fit. I enjoy what I am doing. I find my work to be very satisfying. In the midst of ministry demands, I am finding ways to sustain my personal well-being. I am not eager to consider some alternative kind of work or ministry.*

A person who is barely surviving: *This ministry is very frustrating. I do not enjoy what I am doing. I find little satisfaction in my work. In the midst of my ministry demands, I find that I am drained. I am doing what I need to, but I would gladly consider some alternative kind of work or ministry.*

While we all may have days when we feel that we're just surviving, a ministry consistently characterized by this feeling is a difficult one in which to continue—difficult but not impossible. God can be a tremendous source of encouragement and strength in seasons of distress, enabling us to persevere in fulfilling difficult ministry responsibilities. As such prophets as Jeremiah found, faithfulness in following God's will does not always guarantee a sense of thriving, though it can bring contentment if we are open to it.

As nice as a sense of thriving can be, personal satisfaction and well-being are not our primary goals in ministry; serving God is. However, following God through serving the church in associate staff ministry positions *can* be a growing and rewarding experience, a source of fulfillment and joy, and not just a matter of survival. The good news is that many people who serve in associate staff positions report that they *are* thriving. Of the veteran associate staff who responded to the survey, 94 percent reported that, according to the definition given above, they were indeed thriving. These 400-plus long-term staff members have described for us what has contributed to their sense of thriving and what we might do to experience it as well.

The Question

What does it take to thrive, not just survive, as an associate staff member in the local church, and how can a person get to that point?

Too many people who begin in associate staff ministry find it to be a draining experience and don't stay with it long. While it is true that some are using associate work as an opportunity to gain experience and skills to move into a senior or solo pastoral role, many others have no such vocational goals. Associate staff ministry positions are where they intend to stay, but over time they encounter significant problems that cause them to leave in frustration. Still others stay but hang on in a survival mode with little joy or satisfaction in their ministry. How did this state of affairs come to be, and what can be done to improve it?

Background on Associate Staff Ministry

In North America, the number of churches with associate staff members and churches with more than one associate staff member is growing. Some denominations list in their national directories almost as many associate staff as senior or solo pastors. These associate staff people serve their churches in a variety of ways. Some focus their ministry efforts on children, youth, adults, families, or general educational ministries. Others serve in the areas of worship and music. Some are involved in pastoral care and counseling, and others focus on administration. Still others find themselves wearing multiple hats, carrying more than one kind of responsibility. Not all of these staff members are ordained. Many are in the process of seeking ordination, but others are "licensed" staff members. Their denominations grant recognition of their gifts and calling to ministry, but for various reasons they do not have full ordained status. In some cases, this is an issue of academic preparation, scope of ministry responsibilities, or gender. Still other staff members are neither ordained nor licensed, but are laypeople who have entered vocational ministry.

Historically, associate staff positions can be traced to "apprenticeship" arrangements in which the "minister in training" learned the ministry by assisting an experienced church pastor in his duties. This type of associate staff arrangement was temporary and intermittent. With the exception of some music staff positions (e.g., organist, choir director), the development of permanent associate staff positions is primarily a 20th century phenomenon. It had its beginnings in the late 19th century with the growth of church religious education programs and in the early 20th century with the development of religious education degree programs to prepare people to become directors of religious education (DREs). These DREs oversaw the educational ministries of a church in much the same way a principal gave leadership to a school.

In the 20th century, as local churches grew and became sensitive to a variety of focused ministry needs, the demand for associate staff members, both generalists and specialists, increased. However, the growth of this ministry field has been accompanied by a variety of stresses and problems. In general, associate staff positions have been characterized by relatively brief tenures and high attrition rates. For associate staff in educational ministry areas, Paul H. Veith, writing in the 1940s, summarized the problems in these words:

> Whereas the missionary has status and security, the professionally trained worker in Christian education has neither. He has only confused standards, inadequate recognition, poor salary, almost no job security, little help in placement if it becomes necessary for him to make a change; and there is a tendency to regard him as superannuated by the time he reaches middle life.[1]

Even today, in comparison with solo or senior pastors, associate staff members tend to have lower status in the congregation, lower salaries, and little job security. The work of many tends to be less visible to congregation members, resulting in fewer expressions of appreciation or support. Some denominations have a policy that when the senior pastor of a church resigns, associate staff members must offer their resignations to the new senior pastor. This practice increases the uncertainty surrounding associate staff positions. The situation varies to some degree from one denomination to another, but many factors work against thriving long term as an associate staff member.

The good news, however, is that many people do thrive in associate staff ministry positions. Across North America thousands of church workers are flourishing in associate staff ministries. It is time we learned from them what it takes to thrive, and how current and prospective associate staff can get past the survival mode and find real satisfaction and joy in ministry.

The "Thriving in Associate Staff Ministry" Study

In 1996, the Louisville Institute, the North American Professors of Christian Education, and Biola University provided research grants for a study of "thriving" in associate staff ministry. The study began with two questions:

1. What are the influential factors and practices that enable people to thrive long term in local church ministry as associate staff members?
2. How can current and prospective local church associate staff nurture these factors and practices in their lives to promote longevity, satisfaction, and personal well-being in ministry?

Although I had served as an associate staff member for 11 years and had developed a sense of thriving in my own work, I did not assume that I knew the answers to these questions, especially for people whose ministry responsibilities and experiences differed from mine.

The first step was to review the literature on associate staff ministries, paying particular attention to issues surrounding ministry satisfaction and career patterns in general. Most of this literature is anecdotal. Previous research has focused primarily on sources of stress and factors influencing ministry satisfaction. While some good leads arose from this review, they were not sufficient for an understanding of the factors and practices that cause associate staff members to thrive.

The plan to develop an understanding of how to thrive in associate staff ministry included two phases:

1. Focus groups with long-term associate staff members in various ministry areas who felt they were thriving in their work.
2. Development of a survey instrument, based on focus group results, and its use with a broader sample of long-term associate staff members.

The results of these two phases were to be analyzed to determine which factors and practices had broad support and which were most important to which types of associate staff members.

This plan took nearly two years to carry out. It combined qualitative inquiry through the focus-group discussions and narrative items in the survey, and quantitative analysis of other survey items to understand better the relative importance to different groups of the various factors and practices.

In the first phase, approximately one year was spent arranging and holding 21 focus-group discussions. Participating were approximately 120 veteran associate staff members (i.e., with seven or more years of ministry experience) from various denominations—people who reported a high level of ministry satisfaction. They were asked to describe the ministry issues they have faced, the factors and practices that have enabled them to thrive, and the advice they would give to others wanting to pursue long-term associate staff ministry. A common core of questions was asked, but as different kinds of issues were identified, divergent follow-up questions were raised and discussed in each focus group.

Because the issues, factors, and practices identified could vary with the types of ministries, focus groups were developed for homogeneous groupings—e.g., children's ministry, youth ministry, Christian education, music ministry, and broad pastoral or administrative responsibilities. Also, because of the potential that different issues would be raised by full-time and part-time staff, and by male and female staff, a few separate focus groups were developed.

Focus groups were audiotaped, and the tapes were transcribed. The tapes and transcripts were reviewed and their content analyzed. Repeated themes and strongly held views were noted. A survey was then developed based on the issues, influential factors, and practices identified by participants. This survey was sent to approximately 750 randomly selected veteran associate staff members in cooperation with the following denominations:

United States: African Methodist Episcopal Church, American Baptist Churches in the U.S.A., Assemblies of God, Christian and Missionary Alliance USA, Conservative Baptist Association of America, Evangelical Covenant Church, Lutheran Church–Missouri Synod, Presbyterian Church (U.S.A.), Southern Baptist Convention, United Methodist Church.

Canada: Canadian Conference of Mennonite Brethren Churches, Christian and Missionary Alliance in Canada, Pentecostal Assemblies of Canada, United Church of Canada.

Most of these associate staff members were ordained, but some were licensed or held their positions as laypeople, depending on denominational practices and/or personal circumstances. More specific details about the survey respondents can be found in appendix C.

The survey sought to verify and expand on the issues and influential factors and practices identified in the focus groups, and to explore ways that these can be addressed by prospective and current associate staff members to increase their longevity, satisfaction, and personal well-being in ministry. It also addressed their recommendations to congregational leaders and ministry supervisors. Associate staff members who identified themselves as thriving in their work were asked to complete and return the survey. An overall response rate of 57 percent was achieved. Details on survey procedures and results are available in appendix C.

The Results: What This Book Is All About

What came out of the focus-group discussions was overwhelmingly supported in the survey results: a clear, strong, consistent portrait of what it takes to thrive in associate staff ministry. A remarkable consistency was evident across ministry areas and in the depth of feeling expressed about the issues raised. The study results revealed that the ability to thrive in associate staff ministry is a complex phenomenon. There is no simple three-step plan to get there. Rather, eight major aspects of the associate staff ministry experience need our attention if we want to move from barely surviving to thriving:

1. The ability to find satisfaction in following God's direction.
2. The ability to develop good working relationships with supervisor and fellow associate staff.
3. The development of key personal attitudes and commitments.
4. The selection or development of a supportive church environment for ministry.
5. The regular pursuit of means to nurture personal spiritual vitality and growth.
6. The development of multiple supportive relationships.
7. Attention to strengthening family relationships.
8. The ability to savor the joys and weather the storms of ministry.

These are the areas that make the difference.

This book begins with an in-depth look at each of these eight facets, exploring what they are and how they can be developed and strengthened. It then examines areas of special concern for women associate staff members and looks at the advice of veteran associate staff members for those wanting to thrive long term. Each chapter concludes with questions for personal reflection or group discussion to help readers evaluate their own situations and needs and to identify steps that may help them move toward thriving.

Two of the appendixes were written for the people who oversee the work of associate staff members and can help develop a ministry setting to encourage them to thrive in ministry—the supervising pastor and the church board. In them I strive to help these key people understand the needs of associate staff members and how to support them in their ministries. Appendix C describes the study and its results in more detail.

May God encourage, instruct, and guide you as you work through the material in this book, and may you find joy and satisfaction in your ministry.

------

1. Paul H. Veith, *The Church and Christian Education* (St. Louis: Bethany Press, 1947), 200.

CHAPTER 1

Finding Satisfaction in Following God's Direction

The power of divine calling is not in how one is called but that one is called in the first place.
—James R. Edwards, in "The Calling"

As a high-school student I had plans to pursue studies in forestry engineering and to spend my life working in and enjoying the wilderness. When I came to faith in Christ, God gave me a new desire to work with people and to help them grow in their walk with God. I did not have a sense of calling to be a pastor or to work in the church, but I did know that God wanted me to work with people, not trees. As I pursued my undergraduate and graduate studies in Christian education, God called me to the church, to serve in developing and strengthening the educational ministries of congregations. This calling was not a dramatic event but a growing awareness and understanding through Scripture, prayer, and life experiences that this vocation was where I was to invest myself.

When I began my first associate staff position, I did so with the conviction that this place was where God wanted me and this work was what I was meant to do. In that first year the work was hard, but there were signs of progress and encouragement from many people. It was easy to feel that this was indeed my calling. By the second year, however, problems multiplied, and it was harder to see positive results from my work. My frustration grew, and I began to wonder if I was mistaken about God's direction. Shouldn't following God's call to ministry be easier than this? The senior pastor and I finally agreed that I should look for a new ministry position, but I was no longer sure what I should be doing. If God had called me to this work, then why was it so hard, and why wasn't it more successful? I explored other kinds of work, but I could not escape the conviction that God wanted me to serve in the church. There was no hope for satisfaction outside God's will, but I needed God's help if I was going to reach a point of greater effectiveness and any sense of thriving in ministry. It wasn't easy, but that help came over time as I strove to be faithful in following God's direction.

Calling: A Foundation for Thriving

God is the one who created us and knows us most intimately, including our personalities, character, abilities, desires, and needs (Ps. 139). Out of great love for us, God has brought us into restored fellowship, calling us to salvation through faith in Jesus Christ, our Lord and Saviour. God has also given us gifts through the Holy Spirit (1 Cor. 12), and has created us for good works that have been prepared for us to do (Ephes. 2:10). Therefore, our greatest satisfaction, joy, and fulfillment in life is to be found as we come to understand and follow God's will for our lives. Going our own way leads us away from God's will, and away from that which can bring us true fulfillment in life.

For the sake of the church and the work of God's Kingdom, God has instructed congregations to set apart individuals to devote themselves to leading and serving the fellowship and taking the Gospel to the world. God has prepared these people and calls them to these tasks, to do these kinds of "good works." It is commonplace for pastors and missionaries to describe an experience or process by which God called them into vocational ministry. For some, it was a clear direction given at a point in time. For others it was a gradual understanding that God wanted them to take on ministry responsibility. Whatever the process, many of these people describe how following God's call, though difficult at times, has been a source of satisfaction and fulfillment for them.

But what about associate staff members? Does God "call" them to ministry as well? Do they need a sense of calling from God to enable them to experience satisfaction and fulfillment in the face of their ministry demands? Do they need a calling to thrive in associate staff ministry? The vast majority of the thriving associate staff members in our study (92 percent) said yes. Several explained how that calling had affected them in their ministry.

While involvement in ministry to others is a call that *all* Christians share (1 Cor. 12; Rom. 12; 1 Pet. 4:11-16), a few are appointed by God to serve the church vocationally in various servant-leader positions (Ephes. 4:11). Theologian and sociologist of religion H. Richard Niebuhr summarized four aspects of "calling" to vocational ministry that provide a good framework for assessing one's own calling as an associate staff member.[1]

The Common Call

The first aspect, the "common call" to ministry extended to all Christians, is noted above. No one has to question whether one should be involved in using his or her gifts and abilities in ministry to others. That is how God made the church to function, each person exercising the gifts that God has given as a means of grace to the Body. For a few this means vocational involvement, but it is a responsibility for everyone that comes with being "members of one another." In this sense, *all* are "called." Those considering associate staff ministry need to consider the gifts and abilities God has given them and how these might be used in vocational ministry. Long-term associate staff who thrive in their ministries report that they have developed an awareness of their gifts, employing them in the types of ministry where they fit best.

The Secret Call

The second aspect is the "secret call," an inner urgency to serve God vocationally. Most thriving associate staff members report that they have a clear sense of calling from God to serve in an associate staff ministry. For some this "secret call" is a general call to serve the church; for others it is focused on a particular area of ministry, such as children's ministry or leadership of music and worship. One facet of this "secret call" mentioned by several veteran associate staff, one that has contributed to their flourishing in ministry, is an understanding that they are called to a support role, not to a senior pastorate. One associate pastor in an African-American church in Los Angeles described how his understanding of a calling to serve in a support capacity helped him deal with other people's expectations.

> *It truly is a calling to be in support ministry. People have said to me recently, "You could pastor. Why don't you pastor? Why*

*don't you call the bishop and tell him that you need to pas-
tor?" And I've told them, you know, "God has called me into
this position." It's critical that we recognize the calling com-
ponent. God can call us into the next level, too. And it's not
about capability. It really is about God's direction. Not anything else, but God's direction. And I've told people when God
tells me to do the next thing, that's when I will do it, and not a
moment sooner.*

The Providential Call

The third aspect is the "providential call" of God, guiding a person through
life in a way that he or she gains the experiences and gifts needed for
vocational ministry. John Newton, the former slave trader who wrote the
hymn "Amazing Grace," served as a pastor for 16 years. During this time,
in 1787, he responded to a request from a man asking how to discern God's
call to be a pastor:

> The main difference between a minister and a private Christian
> seems to consist in these ministerial gifts which are imparted to
> him, not for his own sake, but for the edification of others. But
> then I say, these are to appear in due season; they are not to be
> expected instantaneously, but gradually. They are necessary for
> the discharge of the ministry, but not necessary as a prerequisite
> to legitimize our desire after it.[2]

Newton took the aspect of providence in one's calling further, looking at
how God not only prepares the individual for vocational ministry but also
provides the opportunity to minister.

> *That which finally evidences a proper call is a correspondent
> opening in providence by a gradual train of circumstances
> pointing out the means, the times, and the place of actually
> entering upon the work. Till this coincidence arrives, you must
> not expect to be always clear from hesitation in your own
> mind.*

The Ecclesiastical Call

The fourth is the "ecclesiastical call"—a congregation affirms an individual's gifts and calling and invites her into a leadership role. John Calvin spoke of this act as a corporate call, a recognition by the church of the person's gifts and God's calling for ministry, and then a setting apart of the individual for a particular service. Calvin stressed that the individual's "secret call" experience and the corporate call of the church serve a complementary function, confirming the call to vocational ministry.

How God's "Call" Helps Associate Staff Thrive

Veteran associate staff members who are thriving reflect on God's calling in the past and present and see how God has used it to direct and sustain them in their ministry. It helps them thrive where they are, doing what they are doing, in a number of ways.

Peace of Mind in Ministry

People serving in associate staff positions in local churches are certainly capable of doing other kinds of work. Given the many choices before them and the limited pay that normally accompanies vocational ministry, having a strong, clear sense of calling helps give associate staff members peace of mind and confidence that this work is what they should be doing. It is important to know yourself, how God has gifted and called you. This kind of knowledge can help associate staff members find contentment in ministry. For some who do leave vocational ministry, the call from God is so clear that they experience a lack of peace away from it and eventually return. For them, peace is found through realizing one's call. One music minister told of his experience of leaving church staff ministry for a time and the reason he finally returned to it.

> *I think for those who are truly called, there is a burning desire to continue in that. I've been on both sides of the fence. I had difficulties in situations earlier in my life and I dropped out. But in those five years that I was not in the ministry, I found*

myself at the church constantly helping in music programs and that kind of thing, trying to get back into the thing that I knew God had called me to do. And there was a burning desire to do that. There is not anything I could do. I was happy with what I was doing, but I was not doing what I knew that I needed to do.

A children's pastor echoes this sentiment, describing her own struggle with leaving and returning to children's ministry.

I would say number one [for thriving in ministry] is a strong sense of call. I don't think I can—in fact, I know I can't—do anything else, because I've tried. You know, I've jumped out of staff positions and church ministry and tried to do other things, but a sense of call is too strong. I cannot stay there without being miserable. I've got to go back to what I've been called to do.

Perseverance in Ministry

Vocational ministry brings with it times of great stress as well as times of joy. Associate staff ministry is no exception. During the times of stress, frustration, and adversity, having a strong sense of calling to ministry can help the associate staff member persevere instead of quitting. Calling that is tested by adversity drives the person to God in prayer, seeking the strength, wisdom, and courage to continue to face the challenge and minister faithfully. In this way, calling can strengthen one's faith and faithfulness. One minister of music described how this process worked during a difficult time in his ministry.

We recently have gone through a real radical change in our church. The minister of education and I sat many hours contemplating the possibility of leaving the ministry or, at least, leaving the church but staying in ministry. We debated and came up with all the right reasons that it's OK to do it. But when we came back to the call, it was a totally different picture. We couldn't get past the fact that we're called to do this even when times are the toughest and you can't see past the next five minutes. That calling is what carries you through . . . for some who might call this a job, it's much more than a job.

Passion for Ministry

Calling can also bring out a passion for ministry that stands strong in the face of adversity, a passion to see God's Kingdom grow and to be a partner in ministry with Jesus Christ. One director of Christian education explained how her passion for ministry grew out of her sense of calling and helped her weather a season of stress on the job.

> *I have a real desire to be involved in Kingdom work. When we went through a time where stress levels were high because of a conflict between the music minister and the senior pastor, the thing that kept me going was not the appreciation of the senior pastor. I didn't feel a real staff togetherness like I do now, but I still felt called to the Kingdom of God and my passion to make a difference in people's lives, a strong love for people and my love for God that superseded all of the tensions and other things that happened to be going on. I could hang in there through thick and thin as long as I feel like I'm in partnership with the Lord. He enables you to do things that, on your own, anybody else would throw up their hands and say, "I quit. I'm out of here, bud." And I had all kinds of people in the church ask me, "Why do you stay?" And it was easy for me to answer that, because I really feel like I'm looking for the Lord. I'm called by him. I feel a passion to be involved in Kingdom ministry and to be a partner with Christ himself.*

Joy and Fulfillment in Ministry

As people pursue the calling for ministry they have received from God, a deep satisfaction and joy can follow. An overwhelming 99 percent of the thriving associate staff in this study reported having a sense of fulfillment that comes from using their gifts to serve God in their ministry area. This does not mean that there is never distress or discouragement, but as associate staff persevere through those times, God helps them find a joy and satisfaction again in the ministry that they can find nowhere else. One Christian education director who juggles many responsibilities in the church and who teaches at a Christian university describes how this has worked out in her life.

> *Something that is really key for me is having a sense of God's call on my life—knowing this is what God wanted me to do and where God wanted me to do it. And that has been the overriding factor in my longevity, I believe, and that is my commitment to doing what I believe the Lord wants me to do. And then also loving, absolutely loving the church, the ministry, the people here, the pastor, and the tasks. I love Christian education. That's my slice of the pie. And as such, I'm responsible for all teaching ministries from children to adults. And I love training teachers and developing curriculum, and all of that. That is really my forte, and I love doing that here.*

Contentment in Ministry

Our society encourages employees to move up the corporate ladder and become "executives." Even in our congregations, associate staff members can sometimes feel pressure to "grow up" and become pastors of their own churches. I don't know how many times I was asked the question, and it was difficult to help some people understand that I was not called to that kind of ministry. This cultural expectation can exert subtle pressure on associate staff members, causing some to feel discontented with their current ministry positions. A strong and clear call can help an associate staff member face those pressures and that spirit of discontent and find real satisfaction in her ministry in the present, instead of anxiously looking forward to some change in the future. One youth pastor put it succinctly: "If you are called to minister to youth, there's no pressure to try to be a senior pastor." An associate pastor from Toronto warns of the dangers of losing this perspective.

The younger generation is being trained more on the business model of looking at stepping-stones and career moves. "I will go to this church for two or three years and then, you know, I'll be able to step up." I really believe that biblically there is no basis for that. When you're called to a ministry, you should be called to that ministry until God chooses to call you out of it. So you don't set yourself up for "I'm here for a couple of years just to put in my time until I get something that I really want." If you have that mentality, you don't normally stay very long. And if you have that mentality, and you have your stepping-stone above what your expectations and giftedness are, you not only don't get there, you get out of the ministry. A lot of the people are out of the ministry because of those kinds of situations.

A Dynamic Call

Not everyone has the same kind of clarity, specificity, or stability to his or her calling to ministry. For some people it is a fairly general call to serve God's church, and the ways this call can be lived out change over time. From their understanding, God has called them to vocational ministry but has not made clear how this calling is to be fulfilled. An exploration of their ministry gifts and opportunities to work in various types of ministry eventually lead to an understanding of how they should minister, but this perception can change with time. For these people, there is no sense of "identity" as a particular type of minister (e.g., youth pastor), but only as one who ministers. Changes in how this calling to minister is to be lived out are anticipated and viewed as normal.

Others experience their call as quite specific to an area or type of ministry, and they may view themselves as "lifers," totally committed to this kind of ministry. Such a calling brings a strong sense of identity and stability. For these people, God's call has a sense of permanence. They may agree that God is free to redirect them in the future, but they do not anticipate such an outcome. Any growth or development of this type of calling is seen as growth within one ministry field, not a move to a new and different ministry focus. Many, though not all, of the thriving long-term associate staff members described their sense of calling in this way.

Still others find that their call is to serve a particular congregation, and their ministry responsibilities change as the church's needs change. I have a friend with whom I play disc golf every week. (If you're wondering what disc golf is, picture a par-three golf course where instead of hitting balls into a hole, you throw Frisbee-like discs at baskets on poles. That's pretty close!) Wayne has served the same church for over 14 years in four different associate staff capacities: junior-high intern, children's pastor, executive pastor, and adult-ministries pastor. His desire is to follow God in service, and God has directed him to serve a specific church through a variety of means.

There is a dynamic element in all these experiences of God's calling. Though God's call to ministry happens in time, it is not merely a historical event to look back on. God's call is a living reality, for God calls us *now* to minister. This means that for some people, their original understanding of calling grows over time. They learn through their ministry experiences, dormant gifts blossom as opportunities arise to exercise them, and new demands draw out new passions for ministry. For others, the growth in their calling is a deepening that leads to new ways to live it out. For example, I know several wonderful youth-ministry professors who began as youth pastors in local churches. Their calling to youth ministry is still vital, but it has become a ministry of reproduction in which they equip others for youth ministry. In all these ways God is at work, confirming, enlarging, or redirecting the call to minister. It is important that we, as associate staff, remain open to follow God's guidance faithfully. As we do so, we will find that the living God is able to strengthen and sustain us in the ministries we carry out, walking us through the difficult times, and helping us thrive in the process.

What If I Don't Feel Called?

As I have said, not everyone has the same sort of experience of a calling, and some people may question whether they have indeed been called to vocational ministry. Others may believe that God called them in the past, but they wonder whether God still wants them in ministry. There is no easy answer, but we must take care not to make vocational changes too quickly. Many people experience God's call through a process of events, with greater clarity emerging as they are able to look back at how God has equipped and supported them in their ministries. One long-term children's ministry director described how her own sense of calling changed over the years, and how that change has affected her perspective and passion for ministry.

> *I think sometimes we hear the word, "I'm called." And that may be used loosely by some people, but I think that in children's ministry you are called. And if you're not, you don't last long term. For years I did the job. I started out, it was kind of like I was there, you know, and they said, "Here, come do this." And I had never even taught Sunday school, and they wanted me to direct. And so for years I went through the motions. My husband was transferred, and we left and came to Dallas. And at that point, I said I would never work in another church because it was the busywork. It was all those things. And God just hit me over the head, and said, "No, I prepared you, and now I've called you." Now, I've been 23 years in ministry, but the last five, I believe I was really called and I'm finally connecting with the kids. And it's a passion. I live it. I eat it. I breathe it. You know, my husband thinks that he is number two. I try real hard to make him think he is not, but you know, really, I just want to serve God with the kids.*

If you are wondering whether God has indeed called you to vocational ministry, take time to review the four aspects of calling described above, reflect on your ministry experience and your walk with God, and take time to talk with fellow Christians who know you well to help you understand how God is working in the present and desires to direct you. Finding a "spiritual director" to help you assess your calling may prove helpful to some.

I began this chapter by describing my own experience of wrestling with my "call" to associate staff ministry. After leaving my first church staff position, I accepted an unexpected invitation to work on staff in another church. Over the next few years God worked to strengthen and equip me for ministry and to confirm my calling to develop and lead educational ministries in the church. I worked with an approachable and supportive pastor and a wonderful group of committed and gifted lay leaders. I began to see how my gifts fit with my ministry focus and what I needed to learn to become more effective. God eventually led me to service in a third congregation, where I found great joy, excitement, and satisfaction in ministry. I couldn't think of anything else I would rather do, even during those times when everything seemed to be going crazy. My sense of thriving in ministry had not come right away, and over the years there were times when I seriously questioned whether I was doing the right thing, but God worked through these circumstances to help me grow to the point that I could thrive despite stressful circumstances.

Taking Inventory: Questions for Reflection and Discussion

Like the remaining chapters of this book, this one closes with questions for personal reflection or group discussion. You may find it beneficial to take time alone to think through these questions, making them a focus for prayer and reflection. It may also be helpful to discuss them in a group setting with peers in ministry. You could encourage each other to work through the questions and clarify what is important to each of you, and what responses, if any, you wish to make. For those who are married, discussing these questions with your spouse may be especially profitable.

Each person has a unique life and ministry situation, and these questions may trigger other issues that would be more helpful for you to consider. Use these questions in ways that will be of the most assistance to you.

1. Would you say that God has "called" you into ministry as an associate staff member? If so, how would you describe that call? How did it come about? How has God confirmed it?

2. How focused is your understanding of your call to minister? What is the scope of this calling?

3. Have you seen God expand or redirect your call to ministry over time? If so, in what ways has it changed? Where do you see God taking you in ministry in the years to come?

4. In the past, how has your calling by God helped you survive the demands of ministry? If there have been times when you felt you were thriving, in what ways did your sense of calling help you?

5.   Are you now experiencing difficulties in your ministry that are extremely discouraging? If so, take time to review your call from God into ministry. Make this a focus for prayer, and ask God to reaffirm or redirect your calling and to provide the strength, guidance, and courage needed to persevere in your situation as long as necessary.

6.   If you are wondering whether your calling is to vocational ministry, with whom might you be able to talk and pray to begin to sort this out, and to understand more clearly what God desires for your life?

May you be granted clear discernment as you seek to know God's direction for your life and ministry, and may you find deep satisfaction in following it.

---

1. H. Richard Niebuhr, quoted in Roy W. Fairchld, *Discerning Your Call and Your Gifts for Ministry* (Louisville, Office of Enlistment and Preparation for Ministry, Church Vocations Ministry Unit, Presbyterian Church [U.S.A.], n.d.).

2. John Newton, quoted in "How Do I Know I'm Called?," *Leadership*, February 5, 1988, 55-56. Newton's response was originally published in 1787.

CHAPTER 2

Working Well with Your Supervisor and Fellow Associates

> *Satisfaction in ministry has been my relationship with the senior pastor. I think to the degree to which I am in tune with the senior pastor is one of the primary factors in whether ministry is satisfying to me or not. It is not as much for me the music-making and the worship leading, as much as it is that team that creates the satisfaction.*
>
> —A minister of music

When I accepted a position as minister of Christian education at my third church, in Bangor, Maine, I soon discovered that I had stepped into a marvelous staff environment. Ken, the senior pastor, was a warm and encouraging supervisor. His dedication to serving the church, his respect for all the associate staff members, his openness to new ideas, his availability to troubleshoot ministry problems, his concern for me as a person, and his commitment to prayer together in our weekly staff meetings made me want to give my best to my ministry there. Ted, the associate pastor, was a seasoned veteran of pastoral ministry whose grace, encouragement, humility, and transparency in sharing and prayer made me feel welcome, and led me to want to grow spiritually and be more like him in many ways. Mike, the minister of music, was dedicated to excellence in his work, creative, and open to talking about the ups and downs of ministry and parenthood. I had just barely begun my work, but already I had high hopes that this would be a place where I could blossom in ministry, if I was willing to give myself to the work at hand and learn to work well with these wonderful staff members.

Long-term associate staff members report that supportive work relationships with their supervisor (normally the senior pastor) and with other associates on staff (if any) are among the keys to thriving in ministry. Healthy and supportive staff relationships can make ministry seem like heaven, even when ministry demands and stresses are high. But relationships with a supervisor or fellow associates that deteriorate into isolation, animosity, or indifference can take much of the joy out of even the best of ministry results.

As good as many staff situations are, none is perfect, and we all bring potential seeds of destruction into our work relationships in the form of our own sinful natures. Great work relationships with a ministry supervisor and other staff members do not just happen. They take commitment, effort, an awareness of those things that nurture or interfere with the health of those relationships, and the willingness to forgive. The issue is not so much finding a great staff to join as it is learning how to encourage good work relations as a priority and acting on what you as an individual staff member can contribute to staff harmony.

The Importance of Work Relationships

Ron had recently come on staff at his church as worship and music pastor. The choir had been working on a particularly difficult cantata and had just presented it that Sunday evening. To Ron's trained ear, it sounded pretty good, but there were some rough spots that troubled him. When Ron arrived home later that night, the phone rang and he answered it. On the other end of the line he could hear the sound of people cheering and his pastor's voice, like an announcer at a baseball game, saying, "It's the bottom of the ninth, the home team is behind, and the bases are loaded. Ron steps up to the plate, and there's the pitch. He swings and connects. It's going, going, gone! What a massive home run! We win!" Ron cheered too and cried, and on the wave of those words of encouragement, felt deep satisfaction in the role he had taken on.

On church staffs, as in most other work environments, much of people's satisfaction with their work is tied in some way to their relationship with their supervisor. One business professor I spoke with went so far as to say that 80 percent of how people feel about their jobs is related directly or indirectly to their supervisors. For most local-church associate staff members, the supervisor is the senior pastor. Over 80 percent of the long-term staff in this study were being supervised by their senior pastor; the rest had another staff member or executive pastor as their supervisor. Whoever the supervisor, that relationship can have a large influence on the environment in which the associate staff member works, and can contribute to or detract from one's ability to thrive in ministry.

Recognizing that conflicts and frustrations can occur in many ways to undermine staff relationships, and that building and maintaining good staff relationships take time and effort, let's look at some ways in which a *positive* working relationship with your supervisor can work to your benefit, turning a church setting into a place to thrive and to become more effective in ministry.

1. The Power of Trust

"Many a man proclaims his own loyalty, but who can find a trustworthy man?" (Prov. 20:6). The most consistent comment made by thriving associate staff members is that their supervisor demonstrates trust in them and believes in their ministry abilities. Over 90 percent of the thriving associate staff in this study identified that this was true of their work relationships with their supervisors, and they rated it highly in its impact on their sense of thriving.

This trust allows them to exercise appropriate authority, make decisions, try new initiatives, and have a measure of flexibility in how they carry out their ministries. This trust is not automatic, and it cannot be demanded by the associate staff member. It is a quality that develops and is tested and confirmed over time. One minister of music described how his senior pastor's trust helped him thrive in ministry.

> *Knowing that you as an associate have the authority to perform your ministry, to make decisions without having to get his thumbprint on everything [is important]. But to qualify that, that only comes with trust. And trust is not given; trust is earned. The way you gain that is, of course, by communicating that you are on the same page and where you are going in the ministry together, and [having] accountability.*

2. The Power of Encouragement and Affirmation

"Anxiety in a man's heart weighs it down, but a good word makes it glad" (Prov. 12:25). Our personalities are different. Not everyone feels the same need for, or appreciation of, their supervisor's private or public encouragement or affirmation. For many associate staff, however, praise or affirmation from a supervisor is a boost to one's spirits and a motivator to continue pouring one's energies into ministries. This may be especially true for associates whose work is not as public as that of others, and who therefore get less feedback from the congregation. For example, I once sang a duet with my wife during a worship service and received more positive feedback from congregation members for that three-minute song than I had had for the last 18 months of hard work as the new minister of Christian education. Fortunately, when I told my senior pastor, he began to take it upon himself to encourage me in my ministry, recognizing that I wouldn't receive compliments from the congregation as readily as he did. This kind of encouragement can come only when there is a good working relationship.

3. The Power of Loyalty

"There is a friend who sticks closer than a brother" (Prov. 18:24b). Few actions by supervisors have more impact on your feelings about yourself and your ministry than the way they respond when you, or your work, is criticized or attacked. When you have a good working relationship with your supervisors, it is easier for them to come to your defense or buffer you from criticism until you have a chance to present your perspective on what has happened. Supervisors who believe in you and are loyal to you in difficult situations take much of the anxiety away as you work through the conflict. One children's pastor described how important this quality was for her.

> *I've been in my job for 14 years at the same church, and there are a number of things that have kept me there—not that it has always been easy sailing. But one is the support of our senior pastor, who really believes in me and encourages me. And without his support and total loyalty, I don't think I could have survived.*

Like trust, loyalty develops over time. As you demonstrate that you are a trustworthy person who exercises good judgment, your supervisor's confidence in you grows, and her willingness to stand up for you in difficult times increases.

4. The Power of Feedback and Evaluation

"Faithful are the wounds of a friend, but deceitful are the kisses of an enemy" (Prov. 27:6). When you have a good work relationship with your supervisor, you have greater freedom to go to him for feedback on your work. It becomes easier to seek his evaluation of your ministry, because you trust his motives and can receive what he has to say as loving counsel. When your work relationships are not going well, you fear evaluations, not trusting the motives or agendas of your supervisor. If you recognize that you need honest feedback on your work and that you can become more effective in ministry, you must work to have the kind of relationship that makes evaluation a growing experience. This point is critical if you are going to continue to grow in effectiveness.

5. The Power of Mentoring

"Iron sharpens iron, so one man sharpens another" (Prov. 27:17). Not all supervisors seek to be strong mentors in the lives of their associates, but when staff relationships are good, some mentoring naturally takes place. When you gain trust and work well with your supervisors, you're in a better position to observe how they function in their ministries, to discuss ministry issues together, and to benefit from their counsel and experience. This experience is especially important for new staff members, but even veteran associate staff can benefit from a mentoring or mutual-mentoring experience.

6. The Power of Partnership in Ministry

"Two are better than one because they have a good return for their labor" (Eccles. 4:9). Another aspect that thriving associate staff rated as a

great benefit was that their supervisors treated them as partners in ministry. They felt that they were part of the ministerial team, not just assistants or hirelings. While the basic ministry and leadership philosophy of the supervisor are key factors, this kind of partnership feeling can never develop when the work relationship between supervisor and associate is strained. Working well together frees the supervisor to begin viewing her associates as partners in ministry; her voicing that perspective can boost your sense of commitment to and responsibility for the ministry. It can motivate you to do your best in your area of responsibility and to take an interest in the ministry responsibilities of others on staff. This mutual concern and support energize a staff and build relationships that encourage each in his work.

7. The Power of Credibility

"A good name is to be more desired than great wealth, favor is better than silver and gold" (Prov. 22:1). A positive work relationship with a supervisor makes it easier for the supervisor to lift up your ministry and give it credibility across the congregation. When the supervisor knows what you are doing, sees your hard work and good results, and shares this knowledge with others in the church, your credibility as a minister grows. This credibility opens the way for you to take new initiatives and introduce different ways of doing things, because the general trust level in your leadership is high.

Responding to Your Supervisor's Needs

When you recognize the benefits that can flow from a good working relationship with your supervisor, the logical question to ask yourself is, "What can I do to help bring this about?" On the one hand, I *could* recommend that as you interview for a staff position you look for a wonderful supervisor who exhibits all the qualities and practices addressed in appendix A. That is probably too idealistic, and ignores an important aspect of how work relationships come about. A great working relationship between staff and supervisor is a two-way effort that develops over time and depends greatly on the attitudes, commitments, expectations, and grace that each person brings to it. Great work relationships are built over time, and each person is responsible for her own actions and attitudes in the process, not the other person's.

If you take seriously the model of servant leadership portrayed in Jesus' life and teaching with his disciples (Mark 10:42-45), then your first concern as an associate staff member is to strive to understand what your supervisor needs and values from you, and then to serve him by meeting those needs to the best of your ability. This approach opens the pathway for a positive work environment to develop and allows the benefits of it to flow into your life and ministry. But what does your supervisor need and value from you? James Berkley, in a survey report in *Leadership Journal* (winter 1986), summarized three major qualities that pastors appreciate from their staffs: cooperation, loyalty, and ability. Other issues have also been identified within this study and are described below. If you will recognize what your supervisor needs from you, and address these needs, you will have done a major part of what you can to develop a positive work relationship that can benefit you both and the total ministry of the church as well. These needs include:

1. Cooperation

Supervisors need to see a cooperative spirit in their staff, or the task of supervision becomes an unpleasant chore, and communication can shut down. A cooperative spirit is shown through words and actions that demonstrate respect, support, and a team spirit. Taking the initiative to ask if there is anything you can do to help, bringing your concerns to your supervisor with a teachable spirit, listening attentively and drawing out her perspectives on issues you're dealing with, all foster a spirit of cooperation. A competitive spirit that seeks to strengthen one's ministry agenda at the expense of other church leaders undermines the supervisor's ability to trust the staff member. Commitment to function as members of a diverse team, and not as competing kingdom builders, is critical.

2. Loyalty

The need for a sense of loyalty is felt by supervisors as well as by their associate staff members. Supervisors need to know that their staff will act in ways that demonstrate loyalty, even when there may be honest disagreement on ministry issues. Such disagreements need to remain matters for private discussion and not become public issues that can divide a congregation or undermine the supervisor's leadership. Talking behind the supervisor's back instead of dealing directly with him destroys his ability to trust you.

Unfortunately, it is also common for people who have complaints about a supervisor to seek a sympathetic ear and to attempt to gain support for their grievances. They may come to you, praising your ministry and criticizing your supervisor's. Even if you privately agree, how you deflect the criticism and redirect the complainer to deal directly with your supervisor is important. There must be no appearance of division, but rather the encouragement for people to deal with conflicts and disagreements appropriately. Your supervisor will value this kind of support.

3. Honesty

Associated with loyalty is honesty. Supervisors need to know what staff members think and feel about their ministries, about decisions discussed by the staff, and about the ministry needs they see. Honest, open communication is critical for people to function well together on staff. A lack of honesty can cause people to put up defenses or shut down communication altogether. This honesty has to do with communication within the staff but is guided by the need for loyalty outside the staff setting. Where disagreements remain between staff members and their supervisors, the staff should not discuss those differences in the congregation, even in the name of "honesty."

4. Competence

Supervisors want to work with associates who have the basic competencies to carry out their ministry responsibilities. Some supervisors welcome the opportunity to help someone develop his skills further, while others want to be able to delegate a ministry area fully to their associate staff and not have to do any mentoring or staff development. It's important, especially if you are a new associate staff member, to know what level of competence your supervisor expects and to what degree he or she is willing to help you develop needed ministry skills over time. If you find that you need more assistance than your supervisor is able to give, you may need to find someone else with experience to whom you can turn for mentoring.

5. Initiative

Competence without initiative may result in little being accomplished. Again, supervisors differ in how much initiative they expect their associates to take and how much they themselves want to give direction and pacing to how the ministry is carried out. Most supervisors expect their associates to take some initiative in their work and not need to be told what to do all the time. This expectation is related to the level of competence the supervisor expects in her associates and the degree of responsibility and authority she is willing to delegate. How much is delegated may change over time as you gain ministry experience and demonstrate a growing level of competence.

6. Trustworthiness

Just as associate staff members want to feel that their supervisors trust them in their ministry, supervisors want to feel that their associates are completely trustworthy. This quality relates to loyalty but to other issues as well. Supervisors need to know that if they delegate a responsibility to an associate, and the associate receives that responsibility and agrees to see it through, that it will indeed be done. They want to know that matters shared confidentially in staff meetings will remain within the staff and not be mentioned outside. They need to feel that their associate staff can be trusted with the resources of the church and the lives of the people entrusted to their care.

Trust is established and tested over time but remains fragile. It is easily broken by careless words and actions. Associates must be conscious of the trust that has been extended to them, and honor it by faithful action. If you violate your supervisor's trust in you, Christ calls on you to ask forgiveness and be reconciled with your supervisor. While forgiveness may be extended, it can take time for the damage done to the work relationship to be repaired and for reconciliation to be complete. While this might seem an impossible task in the secular business community, within the Body of Christ we have

Christ as our example of one who extends grace and who reconciles us to God and to each other.

7. Open Communication

One youth pastor described the attitude of many supervisors when he quoted his own supervisor's words to him about communication.

> *All I ask is that you keep me informed. I don't like surprises. So don't throw a surprise curve ball down my way. Just keep me informed.*

Supervisors need to know what's happening in their associate's ministry areas, especially new program initiatives, changes, and anything that affects other ministry areas. They don't want to be caught unaware of what their associate is doing. Supervisors vary in the level of detail that they want to know, so it's best to discuss this preference with your supervisor ahead of time. In general, it is better to err on the side of too much information rather than too little.

Supervisors should also understand your needs so they can determine how best to respond to them. You need to speak openly about what will help you be more effective in your work.

While all seven needs are important to developing good staff relationships with a supervisor, some supervisors will be more sensitive to some areas than others, owing to past experiences and current situations. It's important to discuss these needs together so that you can best understand how to serve your supervisor and flourish in your ministry area as well.

Working with Fellow Associates

While your relationship with your supervisor is a critical factor for thriving in ministry, your work relationships with other associate staff members are also important. Whether you work closely together on common tasks, or each have your own separate area of responsibility, you have the opportunity to create a supportive work environment where each associate can benefit from the interest, wisdom, and assistance of others in the group.

Being part of a larger "ministry team" provides a sense of belonging, security, and support, and can be an important factor in your thriving in ministry. (In many cases, this larger ministry team may include key lay leaders as well as other associate staff members.) This kind of relationship does not come about automatically. Too often associate staff members treat each other as competitors, instead of seeing each other as teammates. Creating this kind of team environment is the result of consistently living out several important team commitments, including these five:

1. Cooperation, Not Competition

I had just begun working at my second church and needed to arrange to use one of the church's buses for a youth event. I checked our reservation calendar and discovered that the minister of music had the large bus reserved for the same date I needed it. Not only that, but he had reserved one or both buses for several other dates over the next few months for choir trips. Suddenly, rather than seeing him as an ally in ministry, I began to see him as a competitor for scarce resources. Rather than talking with him about working out schedule conflicts, I began to plan my activities far ahead so I could be sure to reserve the buses before he did. It's amazing how selfish and stupid I could become over a bus!

The first and major overarching commitment in working with other associates is to develop a spirit and mindset of cooperation and partnership, not competition. A competitive spirit focuses on *my* ministry, while a cooperative spirit focuses on *our* ministry. A competitive spirit is unsettling to all involved, creating a climate of suspicion and making fellowship in ministry difficult to attain. A cooperative spirit and the harmony that develops as you work together encourage longevity and satisfaction in ministry. One children's ministry director described the impact of harmony on her work relationships with fellow staff members.

> *If there is harmony on staff, then that can really extend the longevity so we don't want to leave. Because if we left, we would just go off and start a used-car lot, sales business, or something together. Sticking together is very important for us because we feel that God has brought us together.*

2. Mutual Concern

Commit yourself to be concerned with the ministries of others on staff and with their personal well-being. It takes discipline to do so, because your heart and energies can be so wrapped up in your own area of ministry. It requires a cooperative spirit and the growth of a vision of the church's ministry larger than your own area of responsibility. It also requires a willingness to open your life and ministry to the interest and concern of others. When you recognize that you are on the same team, your interest in and concern for the ministries of others are able to grow. A director of Christian education describes how this attitude has affected his own longevity in ministry.

> *A big thing that has kept me [here] is the sense that we're all in it together, really interested in each other's ministries. I'm free to absolutely lead without [others] asking questions in my area, but there is such support there. And I'm just as interested in the youth ministry and in the adult ministry. We're just all building up each other's ministry.*

This aim has not always been easy for me to live out. When the pressure in my own ministry area or personal life is great, I too easily focus inward and lose sight of my role as part of a larger team. I was lovingly confronted one day at a staff meeting when I had finished my agenda items and the associate pastor began to raise some issues in his ministry area. I asked to be excused to get back to work on something, and he pointed out that he had patiently sat and listened to me discuss my ministry needs many times and that he valued my perspective and input as he wrestled with his. His words brought me up short and gave me a renewed understanding of what it meant to be partners together on a ministry team.

3. Mutual Encouragement

As you recognize that you are teammates, and your concern for others' ministries and personal well-being grows, it becomes more natural to encourage and lift each other up in times of difficulty. Encouraging each other when the ministry is not going well and listening to each others' personal struggles are important elements in building up our teammates in ministry. A youth pastor explained how this kind of encouragement affected him in ministry.

> *We're all supportive of one another. When we meet together, if something happens, if somebody dropped the ball, we don't point the finger and say, "You blew it." We all carry it together. It's such a team and such a family, which is incredible. You don't kick the son or the daughter out of the house because they blew it one time. We're there, supportive of one another, encouraging one another. "How can we get through this together?" I think that's a sign of a healthy organization, a healthy church, and that's nice to be a part of something like that. I'm privileged to be a part of a great church that's like that.*

A women's ministry staff member described the personal impact of the concern of others on staff for her, not only her ministry area:

> *We have a large staff. There are about 22 of us. So when we get together, we sometimes give the instruction when we are ready to pray, "Let this be personal. Let's don't get off on our ministries." When we are worshipping, we'll say, "Keep the ministry things out of this. Let's come and let's be personal with this." So we have a time for that in our staff meeting. I feel like every one of those men are my brothers. When I came along there were 12 of us. I felt like I gained 11 brothers. You can't be close to all 11 of them all the same. So I have a couple of them that if I am hurting with something, I'll go to their office, or they'll go by my door and I'll invite them in. Then I can stop and pray with or just talk with them, be really bottom-line with them [about] where I'm hurting.*

4. Mutual Aid

A natural result of mutual concern and encouragement is the offering of aid to each other when there are ministry needs. While each staff member is to carry his or her own workload, at times we need the assistance of others to handle a sudden increase in ministry demands. The willingness to help grows out of a "teammate's" vision of ministry, an awareness of each others' needs, and a commitment to each other's success in ministry. One director of Christian education put it quite simply:

> *Everybody [needs help] at different times. When the crunch is on for a particular staff person, people are there for that person to make sure that it all comes together.*

A youth pastor described how this kind of mutual assistance and concern helped sustain him through some difficult times in ministry. In his case, the concern and help came primarily from lay leaders closely involved with the work of the church staff.

> *But when you do have the staff or the church board behind you supporting you. . . . Like at the church I'm at now, the chairman of the church said, "I've got your back covered. I'm going to be there supporting you and going to bat for you anytime you need it. And I'm going to be praying for you." And I have people from the church constantly calling me saying that they're praying for me and encouraging me in the youth ministry. We just had a youth closely related to our youth group commit suicide. And then right after that we had a girl that was in a severe car wreck and her face was mangled and we didn't think that she was going to live. And these things happened back to back, and it was just a horrid time for us. And it's those times that the church members are calling me saying, "Mike, I'm praying for you. I know you've got a tough job ahead of you with the funeral and with the other girl." And the chairman of the board said the same thing: "If you need me to cover for you for anything, I've got it." And so that really helps.*

The willingness to invest time and energy to help your teammates builds a climate that makes ministry together a joy. When ministry successes come, they are "our" cause to praise God, not just yours.

5. Mutual Mentoring

One thing that I expected as I ministered in a multiple-staff church was that I would learn from my supervisor and from others on staff with more ministry experience. What caught me by surprise were the times when one of them learned something from me. One day our associate pastor, a man in his mid-60s, commented that he was learning from me about caring for one's family while in ministry. It was a humbling experience, because I had been learning so much from him about grace, transparency, and striving for purity in my life.

Mutual mentoring among associate staff members is one of the great blessings of serving with others on staff. As you minister with others and strive for supportive work relationships together, you will have many opportunities to learn from them and possibly teach them as well. When you make this a commitment together, you seek ways to learn from each other the skills, attitudes, and information that will make each of you more effective.

Taking Inventory: Questions for Reflection and Discussion

With all that has been addressed in this chapter, there may be several issues for you to reflect on, depending on your current situation. Look over the lists that follow, and take time to reflect prayerfully on the appropriate questions, or to discuss them with someone who can help you think them through.

If You Are Looking for an Associate Staff Position

While every work relationship develops over time, it may be helpful to consider what you really need from your potential supervisor to serve well and grow in your ministry responsibilities. The better you understand yourself and your potential supervisor, the easier it will be to identify an appropriate fit for ministry. Here are some factors to consider:

1. Some personality instruments, such as Myers-Briggs, DISC, Personal Style Inventory, and 16 Personality Factors, can help you identify how you tend to interact with others in a work setting. Some churches use one of these, or a similar instrument, in the interview process. Even if they don't,

you might benefit from using one yourself so you can be more aware of your strengths, limitations, and tendencies. Check with a seminary or denominational ministry placement center to see what its experts recommend.

2. Don't be passive in the interview process, but actively and tactfully try to learn what is important to the supervisor and what he or she is looking for in a candidate for this ministry position. A job description generally does not address this type of issue well enough.

3. Read and reflect on the next set of questions, not as a present reality but as a look at future ministry. What areas do you think could be stumbling blocks for you? To whom can you turn to talk through the areas you are not sure about?

Questions to Consider About Yourself

Think through your responses to these questions and their implications for working with your supervisor:

1. Do I serve in my ministry position with a cooperative spirit and a broad perspective of the church's ministry, not just focusing on the needs of my own ministry area?

2. Do I demonstrate loyalty to my supervisor, and if there are areas of disagreement, do I work to resolve them in private?

3. Am I open and honest in talking with my supervisor, not trying to push him or her to respond, but encouraging better understanding and seeking to assist in resolving hurts, conflicts, or disagreements?

4. Do I work hard in my ministry, striving to grow in ministry skills and competence, and to take on the level of initiative I have accepted from my supervisor?

5. Am I a person of integrity in my work, trustworthy with the resources and people I have responsibility for? If I need help in fulfilling my responsibilities, do I seek it?

6. How do I feel about being accountable to someone else for my ministry?

Is there anything in my attitude toward authority or accountability that I need God's help to resolve?

7. What kinds of things am I hoping my supervisor will be able to do to help me grow in my ministry? Have I found a way to communicate these things to her?

8. Do I regularly pray for my supervisor, that God would strengthen and guide him in ministry?

Questions to Discuss with Your Supervisor

Here are some questions that could be profitable to discuss with your supervisor. Strive to listen carefully, ask good follow-up questions, and see what you can learn about working well with your supervisor.

1. What three to five things could I do that would help you most as my supervisor?

2. What level of initiative do you want me to take as an associate in ministry, and in what kinds of situations do you want me to check with you first before taking action?

3. If you and I have disagreements about ministry issues, how would you like me to bring these to you and work them through with you?

4. What kinds of things could we do that would help in building a cooperative ministry together?

5. What three to five things do we need to discuss together to help me serve well and grow in ministry competence?

6. Are there any areas where one or the other of us has felt that trust or loyalty in our work relationship has been compromised? Has anything taken place that has caused our respect for each other to suffer? If so, what can we do to resolve the situation?

Questions about Fellow Associate Staff Members

Finally, if there are other associate staff members at your church, here are some items to think about or to discuss with them that could strengthen your working well as a ministry team.

1. What signs do I see that we are serving together with a cooperative spirit? What signs of unhealthy competition do I see? What's my role in moving toward a more cooperative spirit in ministry?

2. Are my eyes so much on my own ministry responsibilities that I have not expressed interest in, and concern for, the ministries of my colleagues? Do we function together as impersonal strangers, or are we expressing appropriate concern for each other as well as our ministries? If growth in this area is desired, what can I do that would be appreciated by my colleagues?

3. When was the last time I encouraged one of my colleagues in her ministry? Am I freely sharing with her the good things I hear about her ministry? What am I doing to build her up?

4. Though all of us have our own ministry responsibilities, are there any areas where I could really use the assistance of one or more of my colleagues because of their gifts, abilities, or experience? Have I been afraid to ask for help for fear it will reflect badly on me?

5. What have I learned from my colleagues in ministry (e.g., about ministry, spiritual growth, taking care of my family)? Have I told them what I have learned from them and thanked them?

6. What growth areas are there to strengthen how we serve together on staff, and what can we do to strengthen our ability to work as a team?

7. Do I regularly pray for my fellow associate staff, that God would guide their ministries and meet their personal needs?

CHAPTER 3

Foundational Attitudes and Commitments

I have learned to be content in whatever circumstances I am. I know how to get along with humble means, and I also know how to live in prosperity; in any and every circumstance I have learned the secret of being filled and going hungry, both of having abundance and suffering need. I can do all things through Him who strengthens me (Phil. 4:11b-13).

When I was a boy growing up, we lived in a farming area of upstate New York. Our ancient house, next door to a dairy farm, had a large uneven lawn with lots of trees. When I reached the age of 11, mowing the lawn became my responsibility. I hated it! The lawn just seemed to go on forever, and I swore most of it was uphill. We had a standard gas-engine push mower that I had to haul around, and I quickly tired of the novelty of it. I wanted to be out riding my bike, playing with friends, or inside watching television.

Now, my father told me that the lawn could be mowed in about three hours, but I knew he had to be lying because it generally took me about six. He offered me a dollar if I could get it all done in one day, but if it took me more than that I would receive nothing. I seldom collected that dollar in those early years. All the time I was mowing the lawn I kept longing to be somewhere else, doing something else. Almost any problem I ran into was enough to distract me from the task. Once I stopped, it was hard to get started again. If I ran out of gas, that was a good time for a break. If it sprinkled a little, I wouldn't mow anymore because the grass might get caught in the mower. If a favorite TV program came on, I would be tempted to take a break to watch it. The more I fussed about the mowing, and the more I thought about how big and unending the job seemed, the slower I worked and the longer it took. I can remember once taking four days to complete the job, only to have to start all over again three days later.

Although I'm sure there were times when my father wondered if he had done the right thing, the responsibility for mowing the lawn remained mine throughout my junior-high and high-school years. As the years went by, I found that when I had some activity coming up that I could do only if the mowing was done, I was motivated to work a little harder and faster. The faster I could get the job done, the less I dreaded it and the harder I worked. I began shaving the time it took to complete the job from six hours to five, and then to four, and finally to three. The job had not changed. It was still the same large, uneven, hilly lawn and the same mower. What changed was my attitude, and that affected my ability to get the job done more quickly, which in turn affected my attitude toward the job. While I never looked forward to mowing the lawn, I no longer hated or dreaded it, and I found a measure of satisfaction in getting it done and doing it well.

Why Attitude Makes Such a Difference

My son, Nathan, attended a junior high school where the administration displayed a banner with a slogan for the students and faculty. The banner read, ATTITUDE IS EVERYTHING. While that slogan may be an overstatement, it trumpets an important truth. The way we view our circumstances, and the attitude we develop within them, is often much more important than the circumstances themselves. Some people, no matter how good their life or work circumstances, still find fault and complain. Others, no matter how bad their situations, remain thankful and hopeful. Our attitude affects our motivation, which in turn affects our energy level and ability to focus on the task and ignore distractions. A positive attitude enables us to persevere in the face of problems and find satisfaction in a task well done. A negative attitude can make even an easy task a chore.

Interestingly enough, when long-term associate staff were asked what helped them thrive in their ministries, they did not just talk about work relationships, helpful practices, and job factors. They also spent a lot of time talking about their own attitudes and commitments and how these contributed to their ability to thrive amid the challenges of ministry.

Attitudes and Commitments for Thriving in Ministry

Thriving rather than merely surviving in associate staff ministries requires cultivating a number of attitudes, and affirming and living out commitments. Long-term associate staff identified and described nine attitudes and commitments that help them thrive in ministry. As you read about them, consider the attitudes of your own heart and the nature and strength of your commitments in ministry. Ask if you need to seek God's help in changing your attitudes and commitments so that you might find greater satisfaction as you fulfill your ministry responsibilities.

1. Valuing Your Ministry Area

To stay with an area of ministry for many years and to find satisfaction in doing it, you need to feel that it is important work. We all want to give ourselves to ministries that we see as significant, valuable to God and to God's people. We need to reach the point of valuing our ministries enough to give them our best effort.

One long-term youth pastor described a change in his attitude that helped him move from "enjoying" what he did to "valuing" it.

> *What kept me going in the early years was my love for kids and being able to do fun stuff. You know, being able to do a cool job. I would get up in the morning and say, "I like what I do. It's awesome, and I get paid for it." That's what it was like in the early years. Now, that stuff is still fun, but now it's combined with seeing that these kids are lost souls. I knew they were before, but now as I mature I'm seeing the impact of my ministry. I see them as lost souls, and then I see the impact I'm having on the kids who come through the ministry now, and it's tremendous. That's what is giving me my second wind.*

Also, the values of the congregation we serve can shape our own attitudes as well. In a previous study in which I was involved, about current and former associate staff members, one factor identified by many former staff members as contributing to their departure was the lack of support the church gave to their ministry area. It seemed to them that their own church did not really value their area of ministry. That was discouraging. It was hard to maintain their own motivation and energy for ministry when the very people they served did not seem to support what they were doing. When you feel that you are in this kind of situation, it is still possible to thrive in ministry, but having a supportive fellowship of people in your area of ministry is critical. We'll take a closer look at this topic in a later chapter.

2. Contentment with Your Ministry

This attitude goes hand in hand with the first. It is hard to thrive in ministry if you find yourself wishing you were doing something else or serving somewhere else. It's hard to give yourself to your work if you find no real joy in doing it well. A spirit of contentment where you are, doing what you are doing, is critical if you are going to find satisfaction in your ministry.

For many people, this point relates to their understanding of calling to ministry. If they are convinced of God's call to this kind of ministry, then it is easier to be committed to it and to find contentment in it over time. However, if their sense of calling is not clear, or if it is focused on some other type of ministry, then it is easy to view their current ministry involvement as a stepping-stone to the "real ministry." One long-term associate staff member described it this way:

> *I think you have to see it not as a stepping-stone to a better career. I know a lot in our denomination for whom it's just like, "I'm going to be a youth pastor for x number of years and then I'm going to move on to the bigger things." But this is* real ministry. *I love my job. I'm a blessed man.*

This spirit of contentment is especially important in serving in a less-visible ministry and being more of a support to the senior pastor. Being number two, three, or whatever on staff can be a test of humility for some. Having the spirit of a servant and being content to serve others in the church and on staff through your ministry efforts are important for your ability to thrive in ministry over the years.

Even if your sense of calling in ministry is clear, your contentment can be undermined by a spirit of pride or insecurity that seeks greater recognition and praise from others. This kind of spirit can cause you to treat your ministry as a career, with a ladder to climb to the top, instead of as a vocation that you fulfill where God places you. Little contentment awaits you if you treat it as a career, but much contentment is possible if you will relax and allow God to direct your ministry path. Eugene Peterson describes the dangers of viewing ministry as a career in *Under the Unpredictable Plant*.[1] I have all of my ministry practicum students read it, and we discuss the need for a vocational perspective. It's interesting that those students with the most prior ministry experience are the quickest to affirm the importance of this perspective. They know from experience the difference this point of view makes in their contentment in ministry.

3. A Spirit of Initiative

The vast majority of thriving associate staff members in this study report that they are self-starters in their work and do not need much supervision. Because of the nature of associate staff ministries, a lot of initiative rests with staff members in fulfilling their ministry obligations. To thrive in associate staff ministry, you need to combine a spirit of cooperation, so you can work well as a member of the ministry team, and a spirit of initiative, so you can give leadership in your ministry area. This initiative shows up in five aspects of an associate staff member's work.

a) As an associate staff member, you need to take initiative in developing the ability to be a good "self-manager." That is, you need to be able to discipline yourself to tackle the demands of the job without close oversight from your supervisor. Using your time and resources well, keeping track of details, and taking care of your own needs in the process allow you to function at your best. You cannot rely on someone else to do this for you; it is something each person must do on her own.

b) Take the initiative in developing a philosophy of ministry for your area and integrating it with the larger philosophy of ministry of the senior pastor and the church. Your ministry philosophy guides and unifies your efforts, allowing you to concentrate on those things that will be most productive for reaching your objectives. However, you need to fit your philosophy together with that of the whole church, or you will find frequent conflicts developing. You need to learn about the ministry philosophy of the senior pastor, the church board, and the church as a whole, so as to fit yours into the larger picture. This task will allow you to support the ministry of the whole church through your own area.

c) Take initiative also in becoming equipped to fulfill your ministry responsibilities. Whatever level of education you have attained, your academic preparation did not address everything you will face in ministry. Much of what you need to minister effectively you will have to learn on the job. To thrive in ministry, recognize your strengths, weaknesses, and gaps in ministry preparation, and find ways to equip yourself more fully. I'll discuss this subject in more detail later in this chapter.

d) Initiative is needed in assessing ministry needs and evaluating current ministry efforts. These responsibilities rest with you if you have taken on leadership responsibilities as an associate staff member. You may want to make this assessment cooperatively with other staff members, but it needs to be done if you are going to give leadership in your ministry area.

e) In light of the ministry needs identified, you need to be able to exercise leadership in initiating change in your ministry area. Thriving in ministry is partly a by-product of seeing ministry successes and finding satisfaction in them. In taking initiative to help your ministry area achieve greater effectiveness, your satisfaction will increase as you see what God does through your efforts and the efforts of those with whom you work.

4. Patience and Perseverance

Associate staff ministries, whatever the area of responsibility, are seldom smooth sailing for long. Sometimes perseverance and patience are needed to overcome challenges or problems. Sometimes you as a ministry leader see the need for change before others do, and you can quickly become impatient waiting for others to recognize and respond to the needs you see. Having patience and being able to persevere in the face of obstacles and disappointment are critical for longevity in ministry and the satisfaction that can come with it. One associate staff member described her experience this way:

> *I have always had that personality that you start something and you finish it. Even when there are tough times, you just stick it through. You persevere. It's not going to be easier anywhere else, and you need to work this out. I've made a commitment to this place, and I'm going to do everything I can and make it work until I've exhausted everything.*

Patience and perseverance are especially important as we face conflicts with others we work with, whether supervisors, fellow associate staff, or lay leaders in our ministry area. Unresolved conflict is one of the major contributors to associate staff members' leaving their positions. Staff members who are patient, who persevere through the unpleasantness of conflict with their supervisors or others, and who find a way to resolve it, are then freed to focus their efforts again on the ministry they enjoy. While this book is not an attempt to address conflict resolution in any exhaustive way, a couple of foundational tips can, I believe, make it easier for you to persevere and find a way through the conflict.

a) *Having a spirit of humility that is not defensive, but open to criticism and willing to listen and to receive correction.* Even if you are convinced that the person you disagree with is wrong, that does not make you right.

b) *Having respect for those you are in conflict with, loving them, and being committed to working together as a team.* Christ prayed for our unity and love for each other (John 14, 17). Paul reminds us of the unity we have in the Spirit, and encourages us to live it out (1 Cor. 12, Phil. 2, Ephes. 4). As difficult as the task can be, these two things need to characterize our attitudes and commitments as we patiently work through conflict and strive for unity in ministry together.

5. Commitment to Keep Growing and Learning

To thrive in ministry requires the willingness and ability to grow, learn, and change to be better equipped to face changing ministry demands. For example, the youth pastor who starts working hands-on with 20 kids and finds the group growing to 50 needs to learn how to develop, supervise, and support lay leaders to meet the demands of an expanding ministry. Or again, the music minister who begins working with the adult choir and finds a number of members interested in forming a small group for spiritual growth and encouragement may need to learn more about giving leadership to that kind of ministry.

Ministry opportunities and demands will change, and you need to commit yourself to keeping pace with the changing needs around you. Over and over again, long-term associate staff members who are thriving in their ministries point to the importance of continuing education and professional enrichment. Ninety-five percent of the thriving staff members in this study identified professional growth as very important to their ability to thrive in ministry. One minister of music had this to say:

> *I've noticed something that has caused other ministers of music to fall by the wayside: It's not being open to change and growing on a constant basis. That's one of the reasons why I attend MusiCalifornia every year. I don't miss it unless I have to. And it's a constant growing experience, constantly changing, new techniques, or methods. If you're not willing to do it, then the ministry leaves you behind.*

There are a variety of ways to keep growing and learning in ministry. Over half of those who participated in this study belong to a professional association and attend regular conferences or other meetings where they learn from others, develop networks together, and receive encouragement in their ministry. Others focus on reading relevant ministry journals and books, looking for new ideas that might be beneficial in their ministry setting. Still others attend seminars, workshops, or courses at seminaries or universities that address issues relevant for their work. Whatever the venue, the commitment to keep learning, growing, and remaining open to change is important for ministry effectiveness and satisfaction over time.

6. Commitment to People over Programs

Over and over again, thriving associate staff members described the need to keep focus on the people served, not on the programs or activities organized and run. While a smoothly running program can provide some limited measure of satisfaction, it is nothing compared to the power of seeing God work in people's lives. Associate staff who put too much focus on the programmatic demands of their ministries can miss out on one of the deepest sources of satisfaction available to them. One youth pastor explained it this way:

> *I've seen a lot of youth pastors through the years, and one of the things that keeps me going is that long-term vision that goes beyond the numbers, that you're here to change lives.*

*And that takes time. I think most of us have been there, we can
get a hundred kids there next week if we want to. But I've seen
too many of my friends or people that I've known get into
youth ministry, and they burn out because it is a numbers game
for them. The ones that I know that have lasted and have
made a difference over the years have been the ones with that
vision that we're going to change lives, not just get numbers.*

Again, this focus relates to your understanding of your calling from
God. Our calling is not to run programs but, through the various programs
and relationships we oversee, to encourage people to come to faith in Jesus
Christ and to become more Christlike. When we lose sight of the end, the
satisfaction we gain from the means is not enough to enable us to thrive in
ministry. The problem is that, amid the daily demands of overseeing ministry
programs, it is easy to fall into the program-focused mind-set. It takes discipline, commitment, and frequent reminders to keep our focus on the people
we serve.

7. Commitment to Investing in Others

Three-fourths of the long-term associate staff in this study reported that
their involvement in mentoring others in ministry contributed to their own
ability to thrive. A similar-size group reported volunteering for ministry outside their local church, helping with community, professional, or denominational ministry efforts. These types of outside involvement contributed to
their overall satisfaction. Thriving in ministry is not just the result of doing
your own job well, but of allowing God to stretch you and teach you as you
invest in others and find opportunities to serve beyond your congregation.

The commitment to invest in others may be especially relevant to associate staff who have been in ministry for several years. Once we have
developed some measure of effectiveness in an area of ministry that we
value, our focus can shift to finding ways to support others who are invest-
ing themselves in the same ministry area. For example, an experienced
minister of music may look for ways to encourage and support newer ministers of music as they get started in ministry. A children's pastor described
her involvement in providing internship opportunities for students:

I appreciate the belief in internship within our church, and I have the privilege of interning young men and women and really supporting them. We say the children are the future, but some of us are getting older in life, and we can't wait for the children to grow up. We need to be producing the next generation of young adults that will have the same passion for ministry with children that we have. Interning students, for me, is very important.

Another associate pastor told how she was affected by a denominational school's using her church to help equip students for ministry:

I know that as I'm beginning to mentor, as I see and meet with a lot of young ministers, I pick up on their energy, and I help them avoid a lot of those pitfalls that I fell into. I think this also helps me stay on the cutting edge of what's happening.

Being involved in ministry opportunities outside your own congregation can be an energizing experience. It can enable you to rub shoulders with others with similar commitments and passions, to encounter the unchurched in your community and to share your faith, to contribute to the ministries of other churches, and to live out your ministry priorities in a larger setting. All of these can stimulate you to reexamine your ministry efforts, your calling from God, and the positive aspects of your own congregational setting.

8. Commitment to Longevity in Ministry

A commitment on the part of associate staff to long-term ministry in their present setting helps create a context that reinforces stability and contentment, and helps the staff member deal with frustrations, challenges, and tempting job offers. This is not a stubborn refusal to consider new ministry opportunities God may guide you to, but a commitment to serve where you are until God makes it clear that a change is needed.

This commitment overlaps to some degree with the development of patience and perseverance. But it is more than an attitude or personality characteristic; it is an intentional commitment to stay put that can encourage you to grow and mature in your ministry setting and begin to see the fruit that longevity can bring. So much of the spiritual fruit of our ministries is "slow-growing" and requires time to see what lasts and what does not. When we make frequent moves, we do not see the long-term impact of our ministry, and we miss out on some of the deep joys that await us. One youth pastor recalled that when he came to his present church, he made a commitment to stay at least until the seventh graders had graduated from high school. He wanted to see their growth and knew that wouldn't be possible if he left after a couple of years. Others say their greatest joys in ministry come from seeing people mature in their ministries and seeing kids grow up into adults who love God and serve others. We will explore this aspect more fully in a later chapter.

A commitment to longevity in ministry makes you think twice before giving up on a frustrating situation, knowing that you will have to live with the consequences. It also helps you resist the tempting offers that may come from time to time to move to a position bigger or higher-paying. It's not that these possibilities are bad things, but they can easily cloud your ability to discern what God desires for you.

9. Commitment to Support Your Supervisor

Making a commitment to support your supervisor and his or her ministry success, communicating it to the supervisor, and living it out serve to build trust and mutual commitment between associate staff and supervisor. This bond strengthens your ability to work well together, making your joint ministry experience more rewarding and satisfying.

I described in chapter 2 supervisors' need for loyalty from their associate staff. Your loyalty and commitment go hand in hand. For some people, loyalty may tend to focus on standing by one's supervisor when he is criticized, and not contradicting his decisions in public settings. Commitment may cover some of the same kinds of behaviors, but it includes a positive, active role of seeking to support and help your supervisor for his maximum effectiveness in ministry. It also means caring for your supervisor as a person, praying for him and doing what you can to encourage him in ministry. This kind of commitment helps build a spirit of partnership and increases the satisfaction you can find in ministering together.

Taking Inventory: Questions for Reflection and Discussion

Together, these nine attitudes and commitments provide a strong base for encouraging longevity, satisfaction, and well-being in ministry. They can help create the context for thriving in ministry. Here are some questions you may want to reflect on or discuss with others to help you evaluate your situation. They may also trigger other questions that would be helpful to consider.

1. If you could put your time and efforts into any kind of ministry, what would you do? How does it compare with the ministry responsibilities you carry now? If there is a significant difference between what you would like to do and what you are now doing, why is that? What do you think God would have you do in the near future?

2. Probably all associate staff members have considered quitting their staff positions and going off to do something else. When do these kinds of thoughts tend to cross your mind? If you have seriously thought of doing something else, what is it? Why have you not gone in that direction? Again, what do you think God would have you do in the near future?

3. What kinds of things contribute to, or undermine, your ability to find contentment in your ministry? How do you respond to them? What help do you need in dealing with things that make it hard to be content? To whom could you turn for help?

4. Do you find it easy to take initiative in ministry, or do you prefer to have more direction from your ministry supervisor? Do you sense a discrepancy between the level of initiative that you prefer to take and the level that is acceptable in your ministry setting? What changes would you have to make to resolve this tension?

5. Do you find yourself frequently impatient or frustrated over problems in your ministry area? How do you deal with these feelings? In the past, have you persevered through a ministry difficulty and seen God work it out? What have you learned from that experience? What might

you do to encourage the growth of patience as you face ministry challenges? To whom might you turn for help with this issue?

6. When you find yourself in a conflict with your ministry supervisor or someone else in your ministry area, what problems have you encountered in trying to resolve it? As you examine your own reactions to conflict, what attitudes and actions have helped you work through the conflict, and which ones have made that harder to do? What help do you need in handling conflicts better? What can you do to get that help?

7. What are you now doing to keep learning and growing in ministry? What resources are you aware of that you have not yet investigated and tried? Where would you like to start, and what encouragement or accountability do you need to see this plan through?

8. How easy is it for you to lose focus on the people you minister to, and to tend to focus on the "program" aspect of your work? If this is a problem for you, what can you do to remind yourself of the purposes you strive to accomplish and the importance of the people you serve?

9. If your ministry is going fairly well, and you think you have some time and energy you can invest outside your ministry demands, have you found any opportunities in your community, denomination, or profession to make a contribution? What opportunities are available that you can explore? Is there an individual you might be a support to, and possibly mentor as he or she begins in ministry?

10. What is your feeling about committing to serve in your present setting for a long time? What problems or benefits do you see? What indications do you have from God about your future ministry? What would it take for you seriously to consider leaving your current staff position? What would it take to keep you where you are?

11. In what ways are you communicating your commitment and support to your ministry supervisor? Is there anything that makes such communication difficult? If so, is this barrier serious enough to cause you to question whether you should continue in this staff position? Is there

someone with whom you should discuss this difficulty, seeking wise counsel on how to proceed? If you have done anything to cause your supervisor to question your support, what steps do you think you need to take to improve the situation?

---

1. Eugene Peterson, *Under the Unpredictable Plant: An Exploration in Vocational Holiness* (Grand Rapids: Eerdmans, 1992).

CHAPTER 4

Church Environments that Enable Thriving

> *Therefore if there is any encouragement in Christ, if there is any consolation of love, if there is any fellowship of the Spirit, if any affection and compassion, make my joy complete by being of the same mind, maintaining the same love, united in spirit, intent on one purpose* (Phil. 2:1-2).

One simple answer to the question of how to thrive in associate staff ministry is "Find a great church setting to serve in." We're all tempted to think that our ministry frustrations and problems would disappear if only we could find the right congregation. Unfortunately, there *is* no perfect congregational setting. Each has its unique mixture of challenges and blessings. Even if there were a perfect setting, that would not necessarily ensure that we would thrive in ministry there. We each have our unique gifts, personalities, limitations, and needs. Each of us has areas in which God wants us to grow. Some of that growth will come through challenges and difficult situations, not from having an easy ministry.

I don't believe that we should seek problem-free churches. It seems to me that God calls us, imperfect servant leaders, to serve an imperfect church, helping it and us grow toward maturity in Christ. As we serve, the church is called to join us and support and honor us in our ministry (1 Tim. 5:17,18). Each setting has aspects that encourage us in ministry, making it easier to thrive, and situations that are stressful or discouraging, making thriving more difficult. Whether or not your congregation has all the features you would like to make your ministry easy and enjoyable, I do believe that it is possible for you to take the initiative and make some adjustments that will help you move toward thriving.

While chapter 3 addresses the attitudes and commitments that associate staff members need to foster if they are to thrive, it seems evident that some ministry settings are more difficult than others. When long-term associate staff members reflected on the effect of their church environments, 11 aspects stood out as making a difference. These are discussed below. Then we will examine the characteristics you may want to look for when you are candidating for a church staff position, and what steps you can take to improve the ministry setting in which you now serve.

Characteristics of the Church

Long-term associate staff described common characteristics of the churches where they thrived in ministry. Their circumstances differed, and not every associate staff member felt that his or her church had to have all these characteristics for them to flourish, but the general picture holds. A healthy and growing congregation that supports your ministry area, accepts new ideas and ministry approaches, and whose lay leaders are committed and dependable is a great place to thrive in ministry!

1. A Healthy and Growing Congregation

At a foundational level, when a church is functioning in a healthy way, ministry of any kind is less stressful and difficult for those in leadership, including associate staff members. This is not to suggest that associates should avoid serving churches that have problems, or that they should look for a new position if difficulties arise. Instead, a healthy church should be a goal to strive for. Everyone in the church will reap the benefits in their ministries when the church is healthy.

A healthy church is characterized by a sense of unity in Christ (John 17:20-21), an evident love for God and for others, especially for fellow disciples of Jesus Christ (John 14:34-35, Luke 10:25-28), and the opportunity for all to exercise their gifts in ministry, building up the body of Christ (Ephes. 4:11-16). A healthy church is characterized by unity in ministry vision and church members who use their gifts to strengthen the body in its pursuit of that vision. It is also marked by patience, love, and forgiveness when there are disagreements or offenses between members. Political maneuvering is discouraged, and people are able to work through hurts and disagreements without bitterness gaining a foothold. While no church may fully and consistently exhibit these qualities, if they are valued by church leadership and present to some degree, the church has the opportunity to grow toward greater health. This health in turn makes all ministries and leadership duties easier. Time and energy are not spent on damage control but used to extend the church's outreach and ministries.

2. Supportive of Your Ministry Area

When a congregation values and supports a staff member's area of ministry, the staff member is likely to feel that what she is doing is significant. We all want to give our time and effort to tasks of importance. Our basic understanding of the importance of our ministries comes from God, but the support of others in the church gives an added boost that can help us persevere in the face of difficulties and calm the nagging doubts that maybe we should be doing something else. When that support becomes practical action, it can provide us with the resources needed for successful ministry. Support for a ministry area can be shown in a number of ways. One is the encouragement and prayer support of the lay leadership. One music minister explained:

> *Having a board that believes in you is extremely helpful—instead of just accounting to them, having them support you. When you're called to a board meeting, when normally you're not there, usually you panic. But then you find out they just want to know about your ministry that night and pray for you. It's so affirming.*

Support can be communicated also through budget allocations for planned activities, opportunities for staff to discuss ministry issues with church leaders, and occasions for staff to communicate with the congregation about their ministry areas. One youth pastor described the support he experienced at his church.

> *Another thing that has been very, very important to me is being in a church that's supportive of youth ministry, not just in theory, but very much so in practice. They let the youth pastor*

be a part of the elder board, recognized as a vital person. I've been involved in churches that allow the youth pastor to have pulpit time to be able to share the vision of youth ministry and then financially backing up the programs and the kind of weird ventures that we want to participate in with our kids. That's been really helpful. . . . Talking to a lot of people who are close to burnout or whatever, I keep hearing from them over and over that "I just don't feel like the church has really supported the youth ministry here." I've been fortunate to be on the opposite side of that.

Knowing that the congregation believes in and supports the ministry into which you are pouring your energy is a boost when the going gets rough and discouragement nags at you. Sometimes the support is there but we're not aware of it. It may take initiative on your part to communicate with others about your ministry so that their support for it can grow and become more evident to you.

3. Open to New Ideas and Approaches

Thriving associate staff members report that their churches allow them to exercise leadership and creativity in their ministry areas. Most associates want to be able to evaluate the ministries they are responsible for and lead in making them more effective. They want to be ministry leaders, not just program maintainers. A church that is open to new ideas offers a supportive environment for the creative associate staff member to take risks and try out new ministry approaches without fearing that failure will result in rebuke or diminished congregational support. This freedom may come more easily once the congregation and lay leadership observe the associate's commitment and faithful ministry over time. One children's pastor described his church's openness:

The church is a healthy church, and it's a growing church, and so it's a very enjoyable environment to work in. They are willing to try new things. But if you try something and you fail, that's OK. We pull up our socks and move on, and try something else the next time. So it's very innovative. I think of all of us on staff as entrepreneurs in our areas.

4. With Committed and Dependable Lay Leaders

One great encouragement to associate staff members is lay leaders who demonstrate commitment to their own ministry responsibilities. These people become partners, united in working together to strengthen the church's ministries. Committed lay leaders strengthen the commitment of church staff. When lay leaders are faithful and dependable in their ministries, they make the work of the associate staff members easier. This commitment by congregational members reduces the stress that comes with vocational ministry.

In Brian's ten years on church staffs, he has deeply appreciated the lay leaders with whom he has worked closely. Many of them have been faithful, going the extra mile to see that needs are met, dependable in attending meetings where there were ministry issues to resolve. Their commitment in the face of competing life demands has inspired him in his ministry. They have been a source of joy, helping Brian persevere when things were not going smoothly. The few times when some lay leaders proved undependable were extremely frustrating and discouraging times. Fortunately, those occasions were infrequent. One blessing of ministry is to work alongside church members who care deeply about the purpose of the church and are committed to serve in ways that help fulfill it. May their tribe increase!

Characteristics of the Staff Position

The associate staff members I surveyed and interviewed identified two aspects of their positions as helping them thrive. Interestingly, both have more to do with involvement beyond one's initial ministry responsibilities than with the demands of the job itself. One's ability to thrive in ministry is enhanced by opportunities to fine-tune the job description over time and to give input into the broader scope of the church's ministries.

A Dynamic Position Description

As associate staff members serve in their positions for many years, they value opportunities to grow and take on new responsibilities. One director of Christian education said new challenges have served as a catalyst for growth in his life and ministry.

*Challenges? Sometimes we look at them as added responsibil-
ity to an already crowded job, but the challenge—you do thrive
because you have to rise to the occasion, and you can grow
again professionally and personally.*

Many associate staff appreciate the variety of tasks and challenges.
Over time, as new challenges come, God draws out new gifts for ministry.
It is not unusual for staff members to discover that they are good at and
enjoy assignments that they had not considered when they first entered
vocational ministry. This kind of growth on the job increases the ways that
a staff member can serve the church. When churches provide for times of
evaluation and ministry needs-assessment that can lead to changes in staff
job descriptions, they encourage staff to blossom in ministry and find satisfaction in how God is directing their gifts and abilities.

Input in the Church's Broader Ministry

When an associate staff member invests time and energy in ministry in a
congregation, he or she naturally develops concern for the church and its
broader ministries. In addition, the longer an associate staff member serves
a church, the more opportunities he or she has to gain insight into the church,
the community, and the ministry opportunities and obstacles. As this concern and insight grow, they need an opportunity for expression, a chance to
help make a positive difference. Thriving associate staff members reported
that there were opportunities in their staff positions to give input to ministry
decisions outside their specific ministry responsibilities. This expression of
confidence in their leadership was an encouragement to thriving in their
ministries.

Opportunities for input come in a variety of ways. Some associate
staff members are able to attend church administrative board meetings and
discuss ministry issues there. Others do not attend this type of board meeting, but discuss broad ministry issues at staff meetings with the senior pastor. Whatever the setting, the chance to help the church beyond one's specific job focus is a rewarding experience that raises the motivation and
commitment to minister faithfully.

Support from the Church

A separate chapter will explore more fully the ways in which supportive relationships help associate staff members persevere and thrive in ministry. One critical aspect is how the support of the congregation is communicated and experienced. A supportive congregational environment makes a big difference for staff. Communication with a supportive church board, adequate pay and benefits to provide for one's family, opportunities for continuing education, flexibility in the work schedule to address family needs, and positive feedback from members all enhance the ministry experience of associate staff members.

1. Communication with a Supportive Church Board

Although not all associate staff members attend meetings of their church's governing board, opportunities to meet with board members and to receive their encouragement and support can make a difference in a staff member's ability to thrive in ministry. Roughly three-fourths of the thriving associate staff in this study do attend administrative board meetings. This presence provides them the opportunity to share what is happening in their areas of ministry, as well as to hear about the initiatives, needs, and issues the board is dealing with that may have an impact on their ministries. It also allows them the opportunity both to be encouraged and to offer support to the board in its work. For associate staff members who do not attend such board meetings, finding other ways to communicate with the board is important. One youth pastor described how his senior pastor helps him.

> *I think a good relationship with your board is important. It always makes me feel so good when the pastor comes out of the board meeting and says, "You need to know that the board said this, or they agreed to pay for this," or something like that, because they felt what I was doing was worthwhile. It was valuable. That has really helped me.*

Other churches establish a system whereby board members are matched up with associate staff members to learn more about them, the ministries they oversee, and the needs they have to carry out their ministries well. This kind of connection to the board is invaluable to many. One director of Christian education described his church's approach:

> *We had a set-up where they assigned elders to each pastoral staff member for a year or so. Not [to] supervise you, but as a friend, somebody that worked with you. And that was really supportive. I think I had an elementary principal one year, and then another time a vice-principal of a high school. Boy, those guys understood administration and education. We really clicked. We met every week for talk and prayer. Those were some significant years when I had the right kind of elder working with me.*

An associate pastor explained how this linkage worked in his church and the ways it benefited him in practical ways.

> *Within the structure of our elders' board, they have set up a liaison with each of the staff people. I've been very blessed to have very wonderful, caring liaisons. They meet with me once a month, and they open the door for me to express whatever it is that I'm dealing with—the good, the bad, the ugly. They support me, and if need be, . . . take it as an issue to the elders' board if it needs some action that requires their endorsement. They have addressed salary, benefit packages— you know, different things like that. I mean they will deal with those issues that can't seem to be brought up elsewhere.*

However it is carried out, the opportunity to share with the board about one's ministry area, and to receive encouragement and affirmation in return, is a positive motivator for perseverance and faithfulness in ministry.

2. Adequate Pay and Benefits to Provide for Family

It is pretty safe to say that people who pursue associate staff ministry do not do so to accumulate wealth. But while money is not a major motivator for associate staff members, it can affect their long-term contentment and stress level, even causing some reluctantly to seek other means of employment. The primary concern is the ability to provide for the needs of one's family.

Because the cost of living varies across North America, the family needs of associate staff members vary. The benefits packages that churches provide differ so much that it is impossible to identify what level of salary is adequate. One helpful rule of thumb is to look at the compensation of school-teachers with comparable education and experience in your community. Your church may not be able to match that scale exactly, but if it can come close, you may find that with other benefits available (e.g., favorable tax status for housing expenses for licensed or ordained ministers), you are able to provide adequately for your family. Don't forget to consider the benefits package that the church is able to provide. Health and life insurance, ministry expense reimbursement, and retirement program contributions are other ways that a church can help meet the needs of its staff members.

3. Opportunities for Continuing Education

Overwhelmingly, thriving associate staff members report that part of what helps them thrive in ministry is the growth that takes place through their participation in continuing-education activities. They report a wide range of activities that help them continue to learn and grow. For some, it is as simple as having a friend or a small group of peers who read the same ministry-oriented book and discuss it together. Others find participation in professional association conferences and workshops beneficial. The benefits of attending these kinds of events can be both professional and personal. One music minister described her church's support for continuing education:

> *The first thing that comes to mind that my church does that helps me is their encouragement for personal growth. We're encouraged to go to conferences and workshops, schools, and stuff like that so we can grow in both professional and personal ways.*

Still others have the opportunity to enroll in formal course work toward the completion of a higher-education degree that benefits their ministry practice. One children's pastor wrote about her decision to return to school for a master's degree in Christian education and the flexibility in schedule that her church allowed to make it possible:

Just the freedom to be able to get additional education while I could still work full time has been beneficial. I don't have to cut back hourly, but I can stay and work full time, and work on my master's program.

You may not have the opportunities to pursue a degree, but having support and encouragement to find ways to grow will help stretch and challenge you. It will help you avoid falling into a ministry-maintenance rut, giving you new perspectives, ideas, and models for ministry. If the money is available, attending courses or national professional conferences can be very encouraging and beneficial. If the money is not available for these kinds of events, then having time to meet with others to discuss journal articles, books, and ministry issues can be a valuable benefit.

4. Flexible Work Schedule to Address Family Needs

There are few real "perks" to vocational ministry, but one of those that is deeply appreciated by associate staff members is the freedom to make adjustments in their work schedule to meet family needs. While some people might expect this to be an issue only for working mothers, both men and women associate staff members value this flexibility, especially in light of the evening demands that ministry responsibilities require. One minister of music described how such flexibility helped him and his family.

We're going on a staff retreat next week, so I needed to move all my meetings to the same week, rather than spread them out. I had a Monday night meeting, a Tuesday night meeting, and a Wednesday night rehearsal, and I had a Sunday night Bible study. By Thursday morning, my three boys were in chaos. My wife was stressed, so I didn't go to work yesterday morning. I stayed home and cleaned the house, did the dishes, that sort of stuff.

This kind of flexibility in schedule can also be seen as a sign of trust, a vote of confidence in the dependability of the associate staff member to do his or her work well. As with other signs of trust, this privilege may need to be earned over time as dependability and good judgment are demonstrated. A youth pastor shared what this kind of trust meant to him and his family.

I like the flexibility of the schedule. I'm respected as an expert in my area, and I don't have somebody bird-dogging me. We have set hours, but if I need to run off and do something, it's OK. My wife is in school right now and we have a little one. There are times when I have had to run home early, or pick my wife up, or even get somebody from the bus station. Nobody hassles me. They just realize that I'm competent and I'm not missing anything.

5. Positive Feedback from the Congregation

One of the greatest earthly sources of joy in ministry is felt when those with whom you minister affirm your ministry and gifts, demonstrate their support and belief in you, and let you know how much they appreciate your ministry. This topic will be discussed more fully in a later chapter, but three aspects need to be highlighted here.

First, a powerful encouragement in ministry comes when those you minister with affirm your gifts for ministry. This is especially true for those just starting out in vocational ministry. Before I could thrive in ministry I needed to see that with God's help I was able to do the work I felt called to do. When you care deeply about your area of ministry, and you want to serve God and the church to the best of your ability, the affirmation of your gifts for ministry is a powerful confirmation that you are where God wants you to be. It is easier to thrive, even in the face of problems and frustrations, when you have confirmation that your gifts and abilities fit well with the demands of your staff position. A youth pastor described why this kind of positive feedback was important to him.

I put a lot of stock in the affirmation of the congregation being the body of believers and affirming my gifts in a certain area. It just really helps a lot.

Second, encouragement in ministry comes when the lay leaders of the church express their belief in you and your ministry and their support for what you are doing. This goes a step beyond the affirmation of gifts for ministry, to the affirmation of you as a leader in ministry. This kind of support and encouragement is most evident when you are facing difficulties in ministry, when things are not going well. Sometimes, when you're not sure that you are up to the demands of the situation, this kind of support can help you see it through.

Finally, encouragement comes when people in the congregation express their appreciation for your ministry. Simple things like a word of thanks and a hug, or a note in your mailbox, can be a big boost to your spirits. This ministry of encouragement can be another confirmation that you are using your gifts in appropriate ways and that God is blessing your ministry. While God's affirmation of your work is most important, God uses members of the church to help "encourage one another, and build each other up" (1 Thess. 5:11). This kind of encouragement can go a long way to help you persevere in ministry and find joy in what you do. One director of children's ministry expressed it this way:

> *I appreciate the support of my congregation. When someone says to you they appreciate you, they appreciate your ministry, they appreciate what you do with their children, that lets you know that you are valued!*

Taking Inventory: Questions for Reflection and Discussion

None of the environmental aspects described above is a "must" for thriving, nor will having all of these guarantee that an associate staff member will thrive in ministry. Each is part of a larger pool of factors that can enhance your ability to thrive. Ultimately, God is the one who works through the circumstances of our lives and ministries and can provide the grace to respond to the demands and difficulties we face. Part of how God does this is through the congregations that we serve. As you consider looking for a church staff position, or as you look at the congregational setting in which you currently serve, there are questions you may want to address as you consider how you can best thrive where God calls you.

Evaluating Prospective Ministry Settings

If you do not currently have a church staff position and are considering a ministry opportunity, the following questions may be helpful as you prayerfully seek God's guidance.

HEALTHY CHURCH CLIMATE

1. Is there a sense of unity in the church regarding its purpose and ministry vision?

2. Do you see an evident love for God and for others by the church leadership?

3. Are people supportive of the ministries of the church and involved in helping to achieve the church's ministry goals?

4. What recent history is there of how disagreements between church members have been handled? Is there good communication among the leaders even when they disagree on what the church should be doing?

SUPPORT FOR YOUR MINISTRY AREA

1. Is support for this ministry area evident in the involvement and prayer support of the congregation?

2. Does the church fund this ministry area adequately to carry out the basic functions and activities that I think would be necessary? If not, have the church leaders expressed a willingness to do so?

3. Are opportunities in place to acquaint the congregation with this ministry area, helping them to see its value and be aware of ministry needs and accomplishments?

OPEN TO NEW IDEAS AND MINISTRY APPROACHES

1. Is the church asking you to come maintain a program, or is it open to your giving leadership in evaluating and strengthening what is being done?

2. As you talk with the staff and lay leaders of the church, do they seem open to looking at new ministry ideas?

COMMITTED AND DEPENDABLE LAY LEADERS

1. Is there a history of rapid turnover of lay leaders in the major ministry areas of the church? In the ministry area you are interviewing for?

DYNAMIC POSITION DESCRIPTION

1. Is the church open to annual evaluations of your ministry, the needs of the church, and possible adjustments to the position description if it is warranted?

2. How satisfied are you with the job description the way it is currently configured? If it were to stay the same for several years, do you think it would be a good fit for you?

INPUT INTO THE CHURCH'S BROADER MINISTRY

1. How important will it be for you to be involved in the broader ministry of the church beyond your specific job responsibilities?

2. Are sufficient opportunities present for you to interact on broader church issues at a board or staff level?

COMMUNICATION WITH A SUPPORTIVE CHURCH BOARD

1. Are opportunities present for the associate staff members of the church to interact with the church's governing board about their ministry areas?

2. Has the church considered assigning church board members to meet, talk, and pray with the church staff outside of board meetings? If not, would they be open to looking at this option if you were to desire it?

ADEQUATE PAY AND BENEFITS

1. Have you calculated the cost of living in the community your church serves? If not, can you get some help in developing a realistic family budget?

2. Does the church provide salary and benefits that would allow you to meet the needs of your family? If not, what other avenues are available to you to make up the difference (e.g., spouse employed part or full time; if your position is part time, finding a second job)?

3. As you consider the benefits offered, are they adequate to address your current and future needs (e.g., health and life insurance, retirement benefits, tax status for housing benefit, ministry expense reimbursement allowance)?

OPPORTUNITIES FOR CONTINUING EDUCATION

1. Does the church support its staff members' participation in some type of continuing-education opportunities on a regular basis? Does it provide the funds and release time to allow staff to attend?

2. If the budget is tight and not much funding is available now, does the church support your developing inexpensive growth experiences, such as peer study groups, auditing a course at a seminary, or attending local ministry workshops?

3. At this point in your ministry, what kinds of continuing education would you benefit most from? Is the church willing to work toward allowing this to happen in the future?

FLEXIBILITY OF WORK SCHEDULE

1. When the workload and time demands get especially heavy, is the church supportive of its staff taking time off for personal rest and time with family?

2. Is there opportunity to adjust work schedules to allow for attending special family events and taking care of family needs as they arise? Is this an important issue to you, given your current family situation?

POSITIVE FEEDBACK FROM THE CONGREGATION

1. Do other staff members at the church report that they feel appreciated and supported by members of the congregation?

Building Support in Your Ministry Setting

If you are now serving on staff at a church and feel that one or more of the areas described in this chapter would benefit you but is not yet a strength of your congregation, here are some questions to consider that might help build greater support for you in your ministry.

HEALTHY CHURCH CLIMATE

1. How can you help reinforce the purpose and vision for ministry that your church leadership has for your congregation?

2. How can you voice support for the broad range of ministries of the church and not just your own ministry area? How can you encourage others to do the same?

3. If you are aware of tensions or disagreements with others regarding your ministry area, how can you work through them with those involved, listening to their concerns and affirming your commitment to unity in ministry together?

4. How can you affirm others for their ministries and help them rejoice in how God is working in your congregation? How can you express your appreciation for them and their ministries?

SUPPORT FOR YOUR MINISTRY AREA

1. In what ways can you share your ministry area with others so they can know more about it, value it, and support it with their prayers? What misunderstandings do people have about your ministry area that you need to address?

2. If you feel that funding for your ministry area is inadequate, how can you present the goals, needs, and plans for ministry for the coming year and help the church leadership better understand the reasons for your budget requests? Is there more you can do to help them understand the value of what is being done and how the increased funding will benefit the church?

Open to New Ideas and Ministry Approaches

1. If you feel that new ministry approaches are needed for your church to accomplish effectively the purposes of your ministry area, how can you begin to help others see the needs you see?

2. With whom should you discuss potential ministry changes? Who is in a position to help you understand how best to introduce the ideas you would like to see implemented?

3. Are you aware of the history of the current ministry approaches so that you understand why they are valued? If you would like to propose changes, how do your ideas fit with the priorities reflected in the current ministries?

Committed and Dependable Lay Leaders

1. Do you affirm others for their faithfulness in ministry and the importance of their work?

2. Does your church have in place means to supervise and support laypeople who take on ministry responsibilities? Is the turnover you experience due to inadequate support for them? What steps can you take, or recommend to others, that might improve their experience?

Dynamic Position Description

1. Are you content with the present ministry responsibilities of your staff position?

2. If you would like to adjust your responsibilities, have you talked with your supervising pastor? What concerns do you think he or she might have? How could you respond to these concerns?

3. Is your church leadership open to conducting annual evaluations of staff and their ministry areas? If you would like to pursue this question, whom should you talk with?

Input into the Church's Broader Ministry

1. How can you take better advantage of any opportunities that

already exist to have input into the broader ministries of the church beyond your own area of responsibility?

2. How can you encourage the church staff to take time to discuss your ministry areas with each other? Are you open to the input of others on staff about your own ministry area?

COMMUNICATION WITH A SUPPORTIVE CHURCH BOARD

1. If you are able to attend church board meetings, do you go prepared with a report to share what is happening, what needs you have, and how others can support and pray for you and those you work with?

2. If you are not able to attend church board meetings, how can you provide a brief report that could be shared with them so they are more aware of what you are doing and how they can support you?

3. Would your board be open to assigning board members to each staff member for encouragement, sharing concerns, and prayer support?

ADEQUATE PAY AND BENEFITS

1. If you feel that your current salary and benefits are inadequate to meet your needs and those of your family, is there an appropriate person on the church staff or board with whom you can share your concerns?

2. Have you sought the help of a financial advisor in the development of a personal or family budget and in financial planning for the future? What recommendations would your advisor make as to how the church could help you meet your needs (both salary and benefits)? How could this information best be shared with your church leadership?

OPPORTUNITIES FOR CONTINUING EDUCATION

1. What opportunities for continuing education do you already have access to? Which ones that you have not tried might be of help to you?

2. How can you communicate the value of continuing-education opportunities to your supervising pastor and your church board? What specific goals could these opportunities help you achieve?

3. If church finances limit your options for continuing education, how might you take the initiative in developing some low-cost alternatives where you are? Who else might be interested in doing this with you?

FLEXIBILITY OF WORK SCHEDULE

1. What are the heavy times of the year for your work schedule? How

might you plan ahead and reserve some special times for personal renewal and with your family?

2. Can you discuss with your supervisor what latitude there might be in adjusting your work schedule to allow you to attend special family events and to care for family needs? What kinds of needs do you anticipate?

3. How can you assure your supervisor and other church leaders that you are adequately addressing the needs of your ministry area?

POSITIVE FEEDBACK FROM THE CONGREGATION

1. What kinds of feedback from the congregation are most meaningful to you? When you receive feedback, do you let others know that it encourages you?

2. If you feel that you are not getting much positive feedback from members of the congregation, have you mentioned this concern to your supervisor? He or she might be hearing some compliments about your work and be able to encourage others to pass them on directly to you.

3. Are there coworkers whom you can ask to give you feedback about your ministry, including both strengths and areas for growth, people who can help you see how God is using you to serve the church?

CHAPTER 5

Sustaining Personal Spiritual Vitality

My soul cleaves to the dust; Revive me according to Your Word (Ps. 119:25).

Of all the advice on how to thrive offered by veteran associate staff members in this study to those just beginning, the most frequently mentioned was taking time to nurture and maintain personal spiritual vitality. It seems that for real thriving in ministry, nothing is as foundational as the quality of our own relationship with God. Thriving has more to do with personal well-being than with the circumstances of our ministries. While our work contexts can make ministry goals easier or harder to achieve, they will not ensure an ability to thrive. But when we cultivate an intimate relationship with the God who has called us to ministry, we have a resource to sustain us through the ups and downs of our circumstances. God is able to provide grace to meet the challenges of life and ministry, peace of mind and heart in times of trouble, and joy and deep satisfaction as we see God's purposes accomplished in and through the church.

Unfortunately, our ministerial vocation does not ensure that our own souls will receive the kind of ongoing nurture and care we need. The busyness and stress of demands facing associate staff members can crowd out the time and attention that should be given to our own spiritual growth. It is easy to feel that because we are preaching, teaching, or counseling others, we ourselves must be growing spiritually. But studying the Bible to preach or teach others does not ensure that we are opening our own hearts to God's instruction. Praying for the needs of others does not necessarily mean that we are dealing with our own spiritual needs. And devoting our efforts to helping others to know and walk with God does not guarantee that we are walking along with them. Eugene Peterson shares this warning in his book on vocational holiness, *Under the Unpredictable Plant*:

> In our eagerness to be sympathetic to others and meet their needs, to equip them with a spirituality adequate to their discipleship, we must not fail to take with full seriousness our straits, lest when we have saved others we ourselves should be castaways.[1]

I know how easy it is to neglect my own spiritual growth while serving in ministry. Over the 11 years that I served on church staffs, I frequently struggled to give adequate attention to my own spiritual nurture. Many times I was so busy providing opportunities for others to come to the spiritual banquet table and enjoy the feast that all I took time for were some bread crusts eaten on the run. Fortunately for me, God did not allow me to continue on that way for long. God used people I worked with; times of worship with the congregation; conversations and prayer with my wife, Patty; ministry and family crises; and the Word to reawaken my need and hunger for a closer, vital relationship. Without this ongoing spiritual renewal, thriving deteriorates to surviving as we go through the motions of ministry, turning our vocations into jobs to be done.

Fortunately, associate staff members have found many ways to nurture their own spiritual growth in the midst of ministry demands. What follows is a description of a foundational attitude and a variety of spiritual disciplines that veteran associate staff have found to be beneficial for their own spiritual vitality and which have helped them thrive in ministry.

Seeking God First: Openness to the Lord's Work

The starting place for all spiritual growth is an attitude of humility before God and an openness to the Holy Spirit's working in our lives to transform us more closely to the image of Jesus Christ. Our awareness of our ongoing need for God's involvement in our lives and our willingness to seek God amid life's demands are foundational for any spiritual growth.

One danger for those in vocational ministry is losing our focus on God's guidance, strength, and grace and beginning to focus on our own abilities, skills, and accomplishments. Pride is an occupational hazard as we receive words of praise and appreciation from others about how our ministry has benefited them. A youth pastor puts it simply and well:

You keep humble and you keep growing. It's very easy to get a Messiah complex. Like it's not going to work unless I do it. That is an enormous trap, not just for any youth pastor but for any senior pastor to fall into. We just need to keep humble.

A commitment to humility and to seeking God first in our lives and ministries calls us to develop a close walk with God. This relationship can be nurtured in many ways, and thriving associate staff members share a number of practices that have been helpful for them. Whatever approaches are used, the focus is on knowing God and being open to the love and direction God provides so that our lives and ministries can be faithful to divine purposes. Another youth pastor described the power of this growing relationship with God for his ministry:

It's my own personal relationship with Christ that renews me. You're up and down, but if I wasn't doing it for Christ, I would have been gone long ago. If that relationship was not built on a regular basis, there would be no way that I could be involved in doing what I've done, because of all the stuff that you have to put up with. To me that's the number-one reason that I keep going on, that relationship that burns every day, that you want to spend time with him. And the strength comes from that.

Personal Prayer: Foundation for Growth and Ministry

One basic foundation for personal spiritual vitality in ministry is spending regular times in conversation with God in prayer. Scripture calls us to an intimate time of talking with and listening to God in prayer. As we experience such communion, God provides peace to our souls.

Be anxious for nothing, but in everything by prayer and supplication with thanksgiving let your requests be made known to God. And the peace of God, which surpasses all comprehension, will guard your hearts and your minds in Christ Jesus (Phil. 4:6-7).

Associate staff who are thriving in their ministries report that praying regularly, either by themselves or with others, has been a powerful influence for their longevity and satisfaction in ministry. Regular times for prayer, talking with God about your life situation and what you are learning or need to learn, and being quiet before God are critical for ongoing direction in ministry and for personal growth. One youth pastor put it quite simply:

I know it sounds like a cliché, but my own quiet times are critical. It's a roller-coaster. There are ups and downs, but there have been seasons of really rich times in the Word and just being quiet where the Lord has refreshed me. And if you don't have that, you are going to dry up. It's as simple as that.

Many veteran associate staff also report that they have a prayer partner, or a small group of people with whom they pray, that is a great encouragement to them. This relationship and prayer support help them to weather the demands of ministry. Some pray with a fellow staff member or a group of staff colleagues. One director of Christian education described how this practice came about on her staff.

When I came on staff, we didn't have regular prayer times together. And so I and the youth minister, over a period of a couple of years, we just forced it into our schedules. And now we're praying together twice a week.

Others pray with their spouse, a member of the congregation, or a small group they attend within the congregation. Still others have a friend, mentor, or group of peers outside the church that they share and pray with regularly. Another director of Christian education explained how she took time regularly with her prayer partners.

One of my prayer partners and I just plan a good part of the day in prayer and fasting every two or three months, and that helps a lot. Most of the time we spend alone and then we compare what God has said to us.

Whatever the setting and whoever the companion, having someone who can listen to our needs, confessions, concerns, and joys and pray with and for us is a great help. For ministry longevity and for personal spiritual vitality, it is important that we have people we can and do pray with.

Bible Study for Personal Growth

Another basic foundation for personal spiritual vitality is spending time listening to God through reading and studying Scripture. Many staff members are involved in Bible study as part of their ministry responsibilities. It can be easy to fall into a pattern of studying the Bible for others, reading it with an eye for how it applies to those we are teaching. I know that many times I felt as if my time studying Scripture to develop curriculum for use in an adult class or youth group was adequate for my own growth. However, if this is all we do, it is easy to miss God's message for us and to mistake familiarity with what the Scripture says for personalized knowledge of its truth and power. Two associate staff members with different ministry responsibilities described how important studying Scripture is for their own growth:

> *You've got to keep growing spiritually. I know sometimes it's easy to say, "Well, I'm in the Bible all the time." But when you look at it, you're studying for this night's Bible study or preparing for this other thing. I need that spiritual growth personally. So I try to set aside a time where I'm not studying this because of the group or whatever. I'm studying this because I need to grow and I need to keep in touch with God and have that relationship.*
>
> —A youth pastor

> *Bible studies are important, not only with groups, but individual Bible studies. Last summer, I did the "Experiencing God" study on my own. Over the last few years I have realized that some of the things that I felt were absolutely necessary to be done are totally unnecessary. And I had given up my guilt about not keeping a totally clean house and all of those things to give myself time to spend in prayer and more Bible study, and developing relationships with people. If I want to spend time in my devotions on my deck for three hours in the*

morning, I do it. I have no guilt about it.
　　　　　　　　　　　　—A children's ministry director

As with prayer, many veteran associate staff report great benefits from participating in Bible study with a group of people, not just on their own. This time with others, without responsibility for leading the group, is a refreshing opportunity for personal growth. For many staff this happens best in a small-group Bible study context. Here they have the opportunity to participate with others in studying, discussing, and applying the message of Scripture to their lives. This is especially important for those who, like this children's ministry director, cannot attend the regular worship services of the church because of their own ministry responsibilities.

> *It's important for me to go on Wednesday night to our Bible study at the church, because on Sunday morning I do not get into the service. I get in for the music part with the special-education class. In fact, very seldom do I get into the preaching service. So Wednesday night is very important. I try very hard to be sure that I am there.*

Whether individually or with others, taking time to study God's Word for personal application is a critical part of maintaining spiritual vitality in ministry. We cannot live off the Bible knowledge we acquired in college or seminary. What we need is time to reread this book that we think we know so well, and allow the Holy Spirit to teach us through the Word, showing us the relevance it has for our life situations, and leading us in responding to God.

Intimacy with God Through Worship

Nurturing a vital relationship with God involves not only prayer and Scripture reading, but worship as well. Whether privately or corporately, our growing experience and knowledge of God should stimulate a response of worship and praise. If our prayer life focuses only on lists of requests, and the fruit of our Bible study is only a growing database of biblical information or lessons for other people, then we are in danger of spiritual anemia. For our relationship with God to grow in intimacy, opportunities must be taken to spend time in praise and worship.

Long-term associate staff members who are thriving in their ministries report that they experience great intimacy with God in worship and that this factor helps them thrive in ministry. This intimacy in worship is a source of strength and joy as they carry out the responsibilities that come with their staff positions. Its importance for spiritual vitality should not be underestimated.

Meeting this need can be difficult for staff members whose responsibilities take them away from their church's regular Sunday morning worship services. For a time, it may be a workable arrangement, but eventually the impact of the lack of participation in corporate worship is felt.

Cheryl, a children's ministry director, started working at a church that had one morning worship service. Because of her work responsibilities, she was never able to attend the service. Later, when the church began holding two services, she still was tied up with work responsibilities and did not attend. For four years this pattern continued, and Cheryl found it to be more and more draining and discouraging. When the church finally decided to hire additional staff to work with Cheryl, it opened the opportunity for her to resume participating in the corporate worship, which provided her spiritual encouragement and refreshment. Now, as the children's ministry staff has grown, Cheryl works with the schedule to ensure that each staff member has the opportunity to attend one of the worship services. She knows first-hand how important it is to maintain personal spiritual well-being in the midst of ministry demands.

Another children's pastor who could not attend Sunday morning worship services described how important singing was to her and how she found another opportunity for that type of worship experience:

> *The worship service is really a high priority for me. I feel that it is also important for me to model this for the teachers I work with. I miss the singing part of the worship service, and that is hard for me. So I joined a gospel choir that meets midweek because I love the music. If I just go and sing on Wednesday night, I'm praising God and I love that. And if I get to sing with them in the jails and sing with them on Sunday morning, that's a plus.*

Along with corporate worship, having times for individual worship is also important. Some associate staff describe how taking time outside in

God's creation or listening to Christian music helps them worship God during the week. These times of reflection on God's greatness and goodness, and our response of thankful praise, help us declare the worthiness of God to receive glory and honor. Worship helps us keep a proper perspective on the God we serve and on ourselves as dependent children. This perspective helps us better evaluate and respond to the demands of life and ministry.

Other Spiritual Disciplines

Along with the three major spiritual disciplines described above, many thriving associate staff members have found a number of other disciplines to be helpful in nurturing a vital relationship with God. These disciplines are briefly described below. The list is not exhaustive but is representative of the kinds of disciplines that many associate staff have found to be beneficial for spiritual development.

1. Personal Retreats

Almost half of the thriving associate staff in this study report that they periodically take extended time away from work, from part of a day to an overnight retreat, for prayer and personal spiritual renewal. These "mini-Sabbaths" for spiritual re-creation are a helpful discipline for restoring perspective, resting, and allowing God to minister to us and guide us. These times apart can be an important tool for ongoing spiritual development in the face of heavy ministry demands. One youth pastor described how he uses mini-retreats to restore his vision for ministry.

> *Periodically I take time away from the church, a couple [of] hours, sometimes three to five. Sometimes I go sit on the beach; sometimes I go up to the mountains. Sometimes I read God's Word for an hour and pray. Sometimes I may sit down and say, "God, I just need to pour out my heart to you. I need to pour out the vision that I'm feeling inside of me, but I don't know how to put it down, and I need to sit with you and deal with it right now in the quietness of the time I have here. I need to work through this with you."*

2. Spiritual Direction

A smaller percentage of associate staff members have individuals they turn to as mentors or spiritual directors. These associates respect the spiritual maturity of their mentors and find great benefit in sharing their life situations with them, praying with them, and seeking wise counsel from them in spiritual matters. Whether one has a formal spiritual director, or a more informal relationship with a mentor, having someone with spiritual maturity listen to our life stories and help us understand how God may be working, and what God desires of and for us, provides new perspective and encouragement to us.

3. Journals

Some long-term associate staff have found that a prayer journal, or other form of journal writing, has been helpful for their spiritual growth. For some, the discipline of writing helps focus their thoughts for prayer, or for thinking through the message of the Scripture passages they have been reading and reflecting on. A director of Christian education explained how he combined a journal with his other devotional practices.

> *I have found the one thing that has truly kept me going and kept my vision was meeting with God in his Word each morning and knowing what he said to me. Writing to the Lord has been helpful, responding to what he said to me in the Word that day, so that it's not just, "Well, I've read my Bible today." I know what God said to me, and that gives me the strength to go on.*

Others find it helpful to write about their spiritual journey and reflect back on it at a later date to see how God is working and leading them. One youth pastor described the eclectic nature of his journal.

> *One thing I do is journal a lot—my own personal joys and pitfalls and struggles. I have a spiral binder that's my journal. Yesterday, someone said, "So how is it organized?" I said, "Organized? It's not organized." It's just kind of there, and if I'm feeling something, I'll sit down and spend some time writing. I have letters to my son in there, I have sermon notes in*

there, but it's kind of my spiritual journey. Just a couple of days ago, on my birthday, I spent some time looking back at the past couple of years of journal entries on or near my birthday. It's an incredible process to look through that and go, "Whoa, I can see those up years and those down years, those up times and those down times." And I can see the faithfulness of God in all of it.

Whether organized or not, writing in a journal has been of benefit to many in focusing their thoughts on how God is at work in their lives, both to transform them into Christ's image and to use them in ministry in the chu: ·h.

4. Service In Other Settings

Some associate staff find that getting involved in ministry in a cross-cultural setting is a stimulus to their spiritual growth. Moving outside their comfort zones, talking with others about how God is at work in their lives, seeing and experiencing the needs of others, and working with others to respond to those needs, open their eyes to see God's work in the world in new ways. The experience gives them a profound appreciation of God's grace to their churches and new visions of how God wants to use them and others in ministry. A youth pastor explained how cross-cultural ministry was a discipline for him, something he did intentionally to keep growing in his walk with God.

You need to keep putting yourself in different experiences and different places as well as do your usual ministry. For example, going on the missions trips and getting in the ditch with a kid and be willing to do that kind of work. We're just back from Russia, and with each mission trip you take, it changes your life.

5. Sabbath Rest

One of the occupational hazards for people in vocational ministry is the heavy work demands they face on Sunday, a traditional "Sabbath" day of rest. While many Christians may be able to take Sunday as a day for worship, rest, and recreation, most associate staff members may find this to be the busiest day of their week. Some long-term associate staff members who are thriving in their ministries report that they intentionally schedule other "Sabbath" days of rest into their schedules, not just for physical rest, but for spiritual renewal as well. A women's ministry director described how this practice had recently become important for her.

> *I have been really convicted for the past two or three months of my need to have a Sabbath. I just have not taken that commandment seriously. I love Sunday, but it's my busiest day of the week. So, to take another day out and have a Sabbath is needed. I think, this is stupid, but I think I operate under the paradigm that "If I'm not working somehow, God is not working." Isn't that arrogant? It's like the height of arrogance. But for me to actually say, "Now, I'm not going to work on this day." So, that's been key for me to take Friday or Saturday as a Sabbath. I'm still trying to figure out all of what that means, but I know it means that I don't work.*

Taking weekly Sabbaths can help renew the energy needed to tackle the problems that come in ministry, helping you avoid burnout. A youth pastor stressed the importance of this renewal for him.

> *I find that if I'm not taking regular times, like on a weekly basis, to have a Sabbath, that the little problems seem to get accentuated somehow, and then something that isn't so big seems huge. So I find just in terms of personal maintenance that having a weekly Sabbath, where you just don't do anything, is important. It's a time of rest, of solitude, listening, reading, praying.*

6. Fellowship

Because associate staff members carry significant ministry responsibilities, and much of their contact with congregation members revolves around ministry needs and planning, it can be easy for them to miss out on the benefits of a rich fellowship with others in the church. Some thriving associate staff intentionally find fellowship opportunities within their churches where they can relax and participate with others instead of being in charge. A children's ministry director explained how this experience was important for her.

> *We have a group we call "Twenty-something." I go to it on Sunday nights. I get my name tag just like everybody else. I usually show up late just because I can, and it's so refreshing. It's also a little strange to not be in supervision of this group. I don't know what they're speaking on a month from now, so it's a little strange for me. The fact that it's strange only reinforces that I really need to be there.*

7. Accountability to Others

Another discipline that some associate staff members have found helpful for their own spiritual growth has been participation in some kind of support and accountability group. This kind of supportive fellowship will be discussed in more detail in the next chapter. Having a person, or a group of people, to whom they are accountable and with whom they can share the struggles of their spiritual journey is a tremendous encouragement. It helps them stay honest with themselves and challenges them to follow God closely in all that they do. A women's ministry pastor said this kind of accountability was difficult but beneficial to her.

> *I stay submitted to others. Yesterday, I and my staff had a prayer time. I had to confess to them something the Lord had really been dealing with me about. I had to lay it out there so they could hold me accountable to it. That's hard, but not doing it is harder.*

Dryness and Discouragement with God

Do people who are thriving in associate staff ministry ever feel spiritually dry or discouraged? Yes! That seems to be a common experience of Christians in general, and people in vocational ministry are no exception. While this chapter has focused on the ways that associate staff members can sustain their spiritual vitality, there is no magic formula or set of activities for making this happen. Anyone who has read the Psalms sees that one's spiritual life can have times of sorrow, pain, and discouragement. While discouragement in your ministry can be difficult to deal with, your own spiritual dryness and discouragement with God can be even more difficult. Eventually, if not faced and resolved, this condition will make ministry more and more draining, causing some to leave vocational ministry or to turn it into just a religious job.

Eugene Peterson describes his own experience early in ministry that drove him to seek a spirituality adequate for his calling both as Christian and as minister.

> In my thirtieth year and four years into my ordination, an abyss opened up before me, a gaping crevasse it was. I had been traveling along a path of personal faith in Jesus Christ since childhood; in adulthood and entering my life work, the path widened into an Isaianic highway in the wilderness, a vocation in gospel ministry. Who I was as a Christian was now confirmed and extended in what I would do as a pastor. I and my work converged: my work an extension of my faith, vocation serving as paving to make the faith accessible for others who wished to travel this road.
>
> Then this chasm opened up, this split between personal faith and pastoral vocation. I was stopped in my tracks. I looked around for a bridge, a rope, a tree to lay across the crevasse and allow passage. I read books, I attended workshops, I arranged consultations. Nothing worked.
>
> Gradually it dawned on me that the crevasse was not before but within me. Things were worse than I had supposed; this was requiring more attention than I had planned on. Unwilling, finally, to stand staring indefinitely into the abyss (or loosen my grip on either faith or vocation, options that also occurred to me), I entered the interior territory in which the split had originated and found heavily eroded badlands. I searched for the details of discontinuity between my personal faith and my church vocation. Why weren't things fitting together simply and easily? I was a pastor vocationally; I was a Christian personally. I had always assumed that the two, "pastor" and "Christian," were essentially the same thing and naturally congruent. Now I was finding that

they were not. Being a Christian, more often than not, seemed to get in the way of working as a pastor. Working as a pastor, with surprising frequency, seemed to put me at odds with living as a Christian.

Like Dives in hell, I was genuinely astonished. I had presumed that the life I had been living personally would issue vocationally into something blessed. Here I was experiencing instead "a great chasm . . . fixed" (Luke 16:26). Like Dives, I began praying "have mercy upon me, and send Lazarus to dip the end of his finger in water and cool my tongue" (Luke 16:24). Unlike Dives, I received relief–but not in a moment, and not without unaccountably long stretches of badlands waiting. Gradually, and graciously, elements of vocational spirituality came into view. The canyons and arroyos were not so much bridged as descended, and in the descent I reached a bottom from which I could ascend as often as I descended (but only after the descent) with a sense of coherence, the personal and the vocational twinned.

Exploring this territory and praying this prayer, I looked for a spirituality adequate to my vocation. Now, thirty years later, I am ready to give witness to the exploration and the prayer. I do it with considerable urgency, for I come across pastor after pastor standing bewildered before the same or a similar abyss. Sadly, many turn back, abandoning their ordained vocation for a religious job. I don't want any of these men and women, whom I count my colleagues and friends, to turn back. . . . Every time one of our company abandons this essential and exacting work, the vocations of all of us are diminished.[2]

If Peterson's experience sounds similar to your own, recognize that God is at work and is willing to bring you through the inner chasms you face. You are called to seek God, to be open to the Spirit's work, so that you may be brought through the chasms and back up to higher ground. Make your spiritual growth and vitality a priority, and as God nurtures your soul, your ministry will flow out of God's work in you, blessing you and those to and with whom you minister.

Taking Inventory: Questions for Reflection and Discussion

While sustaining personal spiritual vitality is foundational to thriving in ministry, there are many ways of pursuing this vitality. Prayer, Bible study, and worship are the major disciplines that thriving associate staff members report as beneficial. Many other approaches can also be helpful. As you read over the questions that follow, take time to reflect prayerfully on them, or discuss them with someone who can listen and help you identify what responses could be most beneficial for you. May they be a stimulus to a closer walk with Christ in ministry.

1. Resolving Tensions

Eugene Peterson reported that after a few years in vocational ministry he saw a chasm opening up in front of him, and found a growing tension between the demands of serving as a pastor and following Christ. Do you find that kind of tension in your own life and ministry? Do the demands of ministry make caring for your own spiritual growth difficult?

2. Prayer

As you look at your current prayer life, do you find that you are taking adequate time to have good quality communication with God? If not, what is crowding it out? Is prayer something you look forward to, or does it feel more like a social obligation that has lost its meaning and joy? If it feels rushed, is there a way to carve out and take advantage of a better time in your schedule for prayer? Would it help to recruit a prayer partner or small group you could meet with on a regular basis to share and pray together? Would it help to try an occasional short "prayer retreat" away from the office? If you are married, how might your spouse be of help in praying for and with you?

3. Bible study

Other than any study that you are doing for teaching or curriculum development responsibilities, are you making time to read and study the Bible for your own life? Are you taking time regularly for devotional reading in Scripture that allows the Holy Spirit to use it to teach and guide you? Are you resting on biblical knowledge gained in the past instead of seeking God through Scripture in the present? If Scripture is the primary way that God speaks to us in the present, how are you making it a priority in your life? Would it help to be part of a Bible study group that you don't lead? Would it help to find some devotional or Bible discussion-guide materials that you can use as a structure for your own study?

4. Worship

Are you able to attend worship regularly in your church? If not, are there alternate services that you can attend, or a small-group worship time you can participate in? In what ways are you encouraging yourself to worship God throughout the week? Is there music you can listen to that may encourage expressions of thanks and praise to God? Can you take time outside to enjoy God's creation and let it be a stimulus to your praise? In your Bible study, can you take time to respond to God in prayer, giving thanks for what you have learned through the Word?

5. Other Spiritual Disciplines

Personal Retreats. Have you thought about taking time for a personal retreat for spiritual renewal? Where could you go? What scheduling would have to be done to free up time? What about a half-day retreat? Who would have to approve it? Would your church help with expenses for this kind of activity? What would you like to do with the time?

Spiritual Direction. Whom have you gotten to know whom you respect for wisdom and spiritual maturity? Would one of these people be open to meeting with you to serve as a spiritual counselor? If this kind of person is not nearby, to what extent would it still be beneficial to write, call, or e-mail to begin to talk about what God is doing in your life and the ways you are being challenged to grow? Is this a kind of relationship you would like to pursue at this time?

Journals. Have you ever tried keeping a prayer journal, or a journal in which you write what is happening in your life and what God is teaching you? If you have, but have not done so in some time, would this be a helpful discipline to try again? If you have not, consider trying it for a few days to see if it helps you attend more closely to the state of your soul and what God is doing and teaching you. If you have kept a journal in the past, take time to reread what you have written, and allow God to help you see how you have grown in the past and ways in which God may want to direct you in the present.

Service in Other Settings. Have you ever participated in a mission project or other ministry in another cultural setting? How did that experience affect you? What did you learn from it about yourself, others, or God? If you have not had this kind of ministry experience, what opportunities are there for you to pursue one? Can you get approval to take time for this kind of service? Can you see benefit to you that you could share with those who would have to give their approval?

Sabbath rest. If Sunday is a busy day for you in ministry, what other time during the week could serve as a time of Sabbath rest for you? Do you feel that you already have adequate time for rest? If not, in what ways could your schedule be adjusted to carve out and protect the time? What would you do with this time if you could have it?

Fellowship. Do you participate in a fellowship group that you do not have to lead? If not, is there an informal group of people you get together with regularly that functions similarly? Is there a group available that you could consider attending? Is scheduling a problem? If so, can schedule adjustments be made to free you to attend?

Accountability to Others. Do you have a person or small group of people with whom you share openly and who can help you be accountable in your walk with God? If not, whom do you know that you would like to do this with?

Dryness and Discouragement. Are you at a point in your life where your spiritual life feels stunted or dried out? Is this primarily a result of a stressed lifestyle and feeling physically or emotionally worn out? If so, an upcoming chapter on balance in life and family may help. If the dryness or discouragement you feel has other causes, you may want to consider finding someone you respect with whom to talk it over, to see if he or she can help you understand what lies behind your feelings. Recognize that this is a common experience, and God may have much to teach you if you will persevere. If you have never read Eugene Peterson's book *Under the Unpredictable Plant: An Exploration in Vocational Holiness*, quoted earlier, it could be a good place to start in examining the origins of your dryness and what might help you through it. Also, consider recruiting a friend or two in ministry to read and discuss the book together. You may find that you are able to encourage and support each other in the process of spiritual renewal.

---

1. Eugene Peterson, *Under the Unpredictable Plant: An Exploration in Vocational Holiness* (Grand Rapids: Eerdmans, 1992), 4.

2. Peterson, *Under the Unpredictable Plant*, 1-3.

CHAPTER 6

Building Supportive Relationships

Two are better than one because they have a good return for their labor. For if either of them falls, the one will lift up his companion. But woe to the one who falls when there is not another to lift him up (Prov. 4:9-10).

One of the strongest and clearest messages from this research is that the ability to thrive in associate staff ministry is greatly strengthened by our relationships with others who support, encourage, challenge, comfort, pray for, and believe in us. We do not thrive well on our own, but we can in the company of others who care for us and come alongside us in various ways. If we are going to have longevity and satisfaction in ministry, we must intentionally build the kinds of supportive relationships that will help us through the challenges of ministry. The associate staff member who functions in isolation and does not have others to turn to for support is in for a very rough ride in ministry.

One of the joys of my own ministry as an associate staff member was the relationships with others who encouraged me when things were going rough and rejoiced with me when good things were happening. These relationships included former professors from college and seminary, members of the congregations I served who worked alongside me, fellow associate staff members from the churches I served, peers in ministry serving in other churches, my wife, and friends from college days. God used these people in different ways to encourage and challenge me. From my vantage point now, it is hard to imagine carrying out my ministry without them. They were stewards of the grace of God in my life, used to help me survive and thrive in ministry (1 Pet. 4:10).

This chapter focuses on the range of supportive relationships outside our family and church staff contexts that help us thrive in ministry. Church staff relationships were addressed in chapter 2, and family relationships will be the focus of the next chapter. As thriving associate staff reflected on the supportive people God had used in their lives and ministries, several types were identified. As someone seeking to thrive in associate staff ministry over the years to come, you will find it helpful to consider the people God has already brought into your life who strengthen you for ministry, and what further steps you may want to take to initiate and strengthen these kinds of supportive relationships.

Veteran associate staff describe six types of supportive relationships that have helped them thrive in ministry. In what follows, several associate staff describe the nature of these relationships, how they came about, and why they have been so beneficial.

1. Friendships Within the Congregation

There is an old tradition in vocational ministry of not getting too close to the members of the congregation you serve, for fear of causing the formation of cliques or jealousies in the church. This concern has led some church staff members to remain distant from the laypeople they work with. Counter to this tradition, over 90 percent of the thriving associate staff who participated in this study reported that their friendships with members of their congregations were a strong source of support that helped them thrive in ministry. Perhaps in a multiple-staff church setting the formation of supportive friendships with congregation members by associate staff is not as threatening to the unity or stability of the congregation as it is if there is only one pastor.

Congregation members can be a tremendous source of encouragement and support for associate staff members. Some of these relationships develop because of the volunteer positions that bring them together to work on a common ministry. Others develop on a more informal level, not because they work together. The support comes in many forms, depending on the need and the kind of relationship that has developed. Friends within the congregation can offer encouragement, sympathy, prayer support, new perspectives, challenges to growth, and even loving confrontation. Here are some of the stories and descriptions of how these kinds of relationships have developed and how they helped support these thriving associate staff members.

> *I moved into a youth ministry department and had three very frustrating years. There were four men on the youth committee, and they became my covenant group. Each one of them had a different task, and if it hadn't been for those four men I never would have survived. One called and told me the joke of the day, the chairman would take me out to lunch every once in a while, and another one would just give support. I think a support group like that is so important.*
>
> —A youth pastor

> *I'm single, so I don't have a spouse or family. I don't live close to my family. For me, the support is friends. There is a couple in the church who are friends of mine. They aren't old enough to be my grandparents, but I call them Pops and Grandma. I can go over to their house and just kick back on the couch. They are sensitive enough to realize that I just need some space.*
>
> —A children's pastor

> *Even though I'm training, mentoring, and helping to develop our lay leaders, they very often have turned around and become my number-one support in praying for me, in caring about my needs and just upholding me. And that has been a real surprise, and a blessing as those people have become real special friends. I think that's one thing that really separates church ministry from a lot of other kinds of work . . . the friendships that you can have with the people who are serving with you.*
>
> —A director of Christian education

> *I found a great deal of encouragement in a small accountability group in my church that was with nonmusical folks, not people that were involved in my ministry. Because of that we could talk about church, but we didn't talk about the details of music and worship ministry. We could talk more about personal things because they are people that I didn't work with*

closely, week in and week out. Just people that I developed friendships with. That was a real strong source of encouragement for me. It took a number of years to find and create that group.

—A music minister

2. Friendships Outside the Congregation

While friends within the congregation can be a great source of support in ministry, there are times when having friends outside the congregation can be helpful as well. When there are difficulties or frustrations in your ministry, you may not always feel that it is wise to share these with others in the church. If they are close friends, they may try to defend you, carrying your frustration on their shoulders and becoming soured on others in leadership in the church. Many associate staff members find that at times they need to dump their frustrations on a friend who is not involved in their church. In some cases, just venting their frustrations helps them gain perspective and strength to go back and work through the issues. In other cases, the person they dump on can ask probing questions and help them identify constructive ways of responding to the situation. Those who are dumped on can often help the associate staff member gain new perspective on the problem, even seeing their own mistakes or faults and how they might resolve the current situation. One children's pastor described how important this kind of friendship is for her.

I dump on my closest and dearest friends. We dump and take turns dumping. I try to talk it through with somebody outside the church that can give me a different perspective. I tend to go to my friends who I feel are very mature spiritually. They give me a godly perspective, godly and biblical counsel because of their background and training. And they don't just say, "Oh, poor Sally, she's just suffering so much." Yes, they're going to say that, but they also say, "All right, you idiot, why did you do thus and so?" They're going to confront me as well as comfort me. That's the kind of person I go to.

Friends from outside the congregation can also be a support to associate staff by providing them the opportunity to escape from ministry problems and spend time with others enjoying nonchurch activities and conversations. Just taking a break from discussing church concerns can be refreshing. One of the senior pastors I worked with enjoyed going duck hunting with community friends who did not attend our church. It was a mini-vacation from the stresses of ministry. A director of Christian education told of the benefits of spending time with people outside the church.

> *We have some friends who are not part of our congregation. Most of our relationships, of course, are with people from the church. In ministry, basically your whole life revolves around the church. Even if you go out socially, generally the subject gets around to the church. We have scheduled times when we can get away with this other couple. I can spout off to them all I want. I can talk about people, and they don't know who they are. And he can do the same thing because he is in Christian work. We don't know who he is talking about, and he doesn't know who we are talking about. We can just spill it all. That's been a help.*

3. Prayer Partners

High on the list of supportive relationships are the individuals or small groups that associate staff members turn to for prayer support. Having someone to dump on is nice, but if that is where it stops, it falls short of the encouragement and support that God has called us to give to each other. Having people to turn to who you know will intercede with God on your behalf is a powerful source of hope, easing the discouragement that can so easily set in during times of stress.

Most long-term associate staff who are thriving in ministry report that they have one or more prayer partners who they share and pray with about their lives and ministries. They can be members of the congregation, fellow associate staff members, peers in ministry in other churches, or mentors in ministry. Different people bring different perspectives as we share with them and listen to them, but all can pray for us and our ministries. In light of the nature of our ministries in the church, this is one of the most powerful sources of support we can receive from others. The associate staff members quoted below describe prayer partners who are a support in ministry.

I have five women who for the years I've been here have been my prime-time prayer support. I just went to them the other day and said, "I'm kind of dry." When I need a teacher, they pray. When I'm down, they pray. When I'm up, I share it with them. It's been a tremendous part of my ministry.

—A children's pastor

Having a personal prayer partner is important. I actually have two that are other gals, one my age and one much younger. Just to be absolutely transparent with them and then pray, cry with them, whatever. Confess or build them up, whichever is the need that week, but it means so much.

—A director of Christian education

I have prayer partners who are both females in ministry. Both of them have really been a support to me in ministry. Sometimes I need advice that's beyond my husband. My husband is so much my "choir" sometimes that he can't be objective. Sometimes I need to hear another point of view. And my prayer partners are very good. They're a very good balance, a good sounding board. Sometimes I tell them stuff I don't really want to tell my husband. And they know how to hold me up in prayer too.

—A minister of Christian education

I learned early in my ministry that I needed prayer support. So in each church that I have been in, I have found three or four people that would commit to praying for me within the ministry so that the spirit of discouragement would not set foot. The spirit of discouragement can really tear you apart. Making sure that I have prayer supporters, people standing behind me that are praying, has been important.

—A children's ministry director

4. Accountability or Support Group of Peers

Most thriving associate staff members have taken the initiative to participate in some form of peer support group. In general, these groups are made up of associate staff from churches in the community who have a similar focus of ministry (e.g., children's ministry, youth ministry, music ministry, women's ministry). Group members gather regularly to share their lives and ministries and to offer support to each other. Some meet weekly or every two weeks; others get together monthly or every few months as their schedules allow. However often they meet, the commitment is to be there to support each other, not just to have some kind of loosely organized community association or luncheon club.

Some groups function mainly as prayer support groups and fit well with the discussion in the last section of this chapter. Others serve as accountability groups, challenging each other to lives of integrity and faithful ministry. This kind of "mutual discipleship" requires a high level of trust and commitment, but the benefits for personal growth and enhanced ministry make it an attractive option for many.

These kinds of intentional peer support groups are one of the most promising trends in associate staff ministry today. They have the potential of strengthening and encouraging thousands of associate staff members as they persevere in giving leadership to their respective ministry areas. This kind of ongoing support is critical for many if they are to ride the ups and downs of ministry. Many thriving associate staff members told how these kinds of peer support groups have an impact in their lives and ministries.

> *In our area we started a little gathering of our children's ministries directors. And for some of us that have been there ever since the inception of this little group, it's a group we can really talk with, talk to, we can share with. We feel it's confidential, it's to support one another. I think that group has been very good for me when I've been in a period of time when I thought I couldn't go on—just because they bring in a different perspective. They ask questions that help you to reevaluate. It's been very good.*
>
> —A children's pastor

Having a support group of fellow DCEs is good, because in some ways it gets you out of your own denomination. You cross over. . . . Your thinking doesn't become just like in a box, like this is how we do it. There are other ways to do it. And it is nice to hear some refreshing ideas from other people and to know also that you could talk about some things that were kind of hard to go through without it really kind of getting to me.

—A director of Christian education

When I was going through training through AME [African Methodist Episcopal] classes, it's a five-year program. We formed a coalition then, and we vowed that we would stick together regardless of what happened or where we went. When it came down to becoming elders, I believe there were six of us left. We're still very tight. We still call upon each other. There have been times, even personally, where we need someone to talk to, someone to cry with, someone to pray with. We all have problems, and we need someone to bounce it off of, and we've always been able to bounce it off with each other.

—An associate pastor

5. Mentors as Models and Counselors

No matter how long veteran associate staff members have been in ministry, they continue to benefit from ongoing relationships with mentors. In some cases, these mentors are people who were instrumental in initially encouraging them to consider vocational ministry. Former pastors, children's or youth pastors, college or seminary professors— each can provide ongoing support and encouragement for the associate staff member in ministry. In other cases, the mentor is a person in the same area of ministry with more experience who encouraged them along after they got started. Some of these relationships began through participation in a local, regional, or national association for ministry professionals. Wherever they are found, the ongoing relationships with these mentors provide support through example, wise counsel, and words of encouragement. Many thriving associate staff members point to these kinds of mentors as one of the reasons why they have made it so far in ministry.

I found at my last church I still have people who are mentors to me from 2,000 miles away. And I see them—they come out here for holidays, or I'll go there for a holiday, and we'll spend a couple of weeks together. I've got one friend in particular that's about 50 years old, so he is somewhat older than I am, and we just go out and backpack for a week. We pretty much take the whole universe apart and put it back together again by the time we're done.

—A director of Christian education

I guess some of the guys that mentored me have been like a father to me—encouraging, comforting, urging me to live a life worthy. And I thought about some of the times I needed a shoulder to cry on and sometimes I needed encouragement and sometimes I needed a kick in the pants. And these guys always just seemed to have the wisdom to give me just what I needed at the moment. And they were very encouraging, or they would give a gentle nudge in the right direction. Encouragement from these guys, 'cause I knew they knew what they were talking about, it meant so much to me. They would see things in me that I didn't see in myself.

—A youth pastor

The pastor and minister of music in the church where I felt my calling to the ministry have over the years been encouragers to me. It wasn't just when I made the decision, but for years afterwards have kept in touch. They wanted to know how I was doing, just encouraging me along the way. When I had a need, I could call them. It has really meant a lot to me to have somebody who cared enough to see me start my ministry and encourage me to finish well.

—A music minister

My college professor was key. She was the primary Christian education professor at this college that I attended, and she is now 82 years old. We still talk on the phone several times during the year. She is in Connecticut. But it was because she was real with me. It wasn't a classroom sterile setting. She had me in her home. It was the belief in me. I mean, I almost flunked teaching the Bible in her class because I was so quiet and shy, but she really believed in me. And now I teach college classes myself.

—A children's pastor

6. Extended Family as Support for Ministry

While immediate family relationships will be the focus of the next chapter, it should be noted here that some associate staff members find that the support of their extended family, especially their parents, is a blessing, and helps them live out their ministry values and persevere during difficult times. Maintaining healthy relationships with extended family increases the supportive resources to help us survive the hard times and find satisfaction as we serve. Those associate staff members who have this kind of support are blessed indeed. Two youth pastors told how their parents were an important support to them in ministry.

For me it had to be my own parents. Fortunately, I was lucky enough to be born into a Christian family. But it wasn't just the churchgoing things. They were always very active and very God-fearing. I can't point to any one specific thing, but their support throughout the years, prayer support, and just their role model of ministering, serving, and caring.

My parents still encourage me, and in times of discouragement they're on the phone and saying, "Hey, Mark, we know that God has called you into this, and we're praying for you." And they're a strong encouragement to me.

Taking Inventory: Questions for Reflection and Discussion

Every thriving associate staff member has his or her own unique mix of supportive relationships, and probably few would say that they have strong support in all six types of relationships. The issue is not the number of relationships, or having some particular balance of types. Instead, it is about having access to high-quality supportive relationships that God can use to help sustain and encourage you in your ministry. You may have one or two such relationships, or many. The point is, we were not made to be alone, either in our ministry or our personal lives.

The following questions encourage you to look at the supportive relationships that you already have and how you might draw encouragement from them. The questions also allow you to identify areas where supportive relationships could be developed, helping you move from surviving to thriving in ministry.

Friendships Within the Congregation

1. How do you feel about developing friendships with people in your congregation? What concerns do you have about doing this?

2. What cautions would you need to take to encourage congregational friends to maintain a positive perspective about the church and its leadership during times when you are frustrated or discouraged?

3. When you talk with lay leaders in your area of ministry, do you keep the conversation focused on business, or do you take time to share more personally and to encourage and pray for each other? How might you move in this direction?

Friendships Outside the Congregation

1. Is all of your time spent with members of your church, so that you have no time to develop friendships with others outside the congregation?

2. Do you feel the need for relationships with people with whom the conversation won't always come around to issues about the church and your ministry?

3. What kinds of community activities are available that you might enjoy, providing you the opportunity to get to know others in your community? (Consider parent-teacher association, community recreation and sports programs, music and other performance arts.)

4. What kinds of hobbies do you enjoy that you might be able to do with others outside your church? Are there organizations around that promote these kinds of activities?

5. How can you free your schedule to have time for relationships with others from outside the church if you feel this would be of benefit to you?

Prayer Partners

1. Whom do you know (or are getting to know) that you could talk to about ministry and/or personal issues, and who could pray with and for you?

2. If you already have people you can share and pray with, would it help to do so in a more deliberate or regular way than you are now? How often would you like to meet?

3. How can you better support your prayer partners with your own prayers and words of encouragement?

Support or Accountability Group of Peers

1. Whom do you know in your community or region who is involved in the same type of ministry as you? Have you had times together to talk about your work and issues you are facing, and to be an encouragement to each other? Would it be helpful to meet on a regular basis?

2. Are there areas in your life and ministry where it would be helpful to have a colleague to help hold you accountable to live out what you believe to be important and right?

3. Is there a local, regional, or national professional organization for people in your type of associate staff ministry? If so, are you a member? If not, look over those listed in appendix D. Through one of these organizations you may be able to connect with others who share your motivation and concerns for ministry.

4.   If there is not a supportive fellowship of ministry peers in your area, but you know one or more people who could join you, why not contact them and begin this type of group. You may find that over time the group grows and helps meet the needs of others in ministry as well.

Mentors

1.   Who encouraged you in the past as you began to get involved in ministry? Were there pastoral staff, lay leaders, or college or seminary faculty who encouraged your growth and ministry involvement? What about people you have gotten to know through involvement in a ministerial or professional organization? How about contacting one or more of them to let them know how God has worked in and through your life, and invite them to respond?

2.   Are there people who have mentored you in the past with whom you've lost touch? If you think they would welcome renewed contact, consider getting in touch and telling them about your life and ministry since you last saw them. If there are areas in which you would appreciate their counsel or prayer, ask if they would be willing to encourage and assist you in these ways.

3.   If someone is actively mentoring you, have you shared with that person how he or she is helping you, and how much you appreciate that help?

Extended Family

1.   If you have parents or other extended family who are an encouragement and support to you in your ministry, have you thanked God and them for their support? Be sure to let them know when things are going well, not just when you have problems or frustrations. Allow them to share in the joys and to praise God with you.

2.   If you think some members of your extended family would be a support to you if they knew more about your work, take time to let them

hear what you are doing, and one or two concerns about which you would appreciate their feedback or prayer. Invite them to give their support, and thank them for the ways they help you. Nurture this kind of supportive relationship that can last a lifetime.

3. If your family is not supportive of your ministry, look for ways to strengthen the other kinds of supportive relationships described above. What person can you connect with who can provide ongoing encouragement to help you through difficult times?

CHAPTER 7

Strengthening the Home Front

If a man does not know how to manage his own household, how will he take care of the church of God? (I Tim. 3:5).

One important area of supportive relationships not addressed in chapter 6 is the associate staff member's immediate family. Most staff members report that this area of relationships is foundational to their longevity and satisfaction in ministry. For associate staff who are married, no other relationship is as critical to the ability to thrive in ministry as the one with a spouse. For associate staff who are parents, this role can bring with it added stress but also encouragement and joy. In addition, being the spouse or child of a church staff member can have its own unique stresses and frustrations, potentially undermining the family's relational health. If our relationships with our spouse and children are foundational to satisfaction in ministry, and if our ability to have a healthy family life faces potential threats, then it is important to find ways to reduce or prevent threats and strengthen our family relationships.

This chapter begins with a look at the ways in which married associate staff members' relationships with their spouses and children help support them in their ministries. It then addresses the potential hazards of family life for an associate staff member and ways to strengthen family relationships. Attention is then given to the single associate staff member and how "family-like" supportive relationships can be nurtured. Finally, the chapter concludes with questions for reflection and assessment. How healthy is your family life as you serve in your church? What could you do to strengthen it?

The Power of a Supportive Spouse

For associate staff members who are married, no relationship is viewed as more important to the ability to thrive in ministry as the one with their spouse. Almost 90 percent of the thriving associate staff members in this study are married, and 97 percent of them identified their spouse's support as a major influence in their satisfaction and longevity in ministry. No other factor gets a higher rating.

Patty and I recently celebrated our 20th anniversary. We married while I was still in seminary and entered congregational ministry in our third year together. For the next 11 years I served congregations in Christian education staff positions, with Patty supporting me and encouraging me along the way. She herself did not often get involved in the Christian education ministries. Her gifts and passions lay in music, and she used them in many ways in the churches we served. Even though she was not my "partner" in ministry most of the time, her support was still important to me. Although I benefited from good relationships with most of the church staff members I served with, and I appreciated peers and professors who mentored and encouraged me, there were many times when I would likely not have been able to continue without Patty's support.

I remember when things were not going well in my first congregation, and the pastor and I had concluded that it would be best for me to resign and look for another position. This crisis was coming at a time when Patty was about to take our infant daughter to visit her parents in Florida for a few weeks. Not having her around while I dealt with the stress of the decision and the aftermath of its announcement was very hard. When she returned, and we walked through the difficulty of resigning, her support encouraged me to look for another staff position and not give up on congregational ministry. It would have been easy for me to turn my back on the ministry in discouragement. I did end up pursuing another position that turned out to be a fruitful ministry experience, and a few years later we made another change to a church where the ministry really blossomed and I had some of my most rewarding ministry experiences. It wasn't all wonderful, and there were many times when discouragement and stress would take their toll on me. Over those years, Patty was my best supporter as I attempted to live out my calling in ministry.

Spouses can be a support to associate staff members in a variety of ways. Below are examples of seven aspects of spousal support as described by long-term associate staff members who are thriving in their ministries.

1. Support in Pursuing Calling

Many associate staff members were married before they considered pursuing vocational ministry. The decision to take on an associate staff position was one that had to be worked through together. Feeling supported by one's spouse in the decision to pursue God's calling to serve on a church staff is a wonderful experience. Knowing that your spouse sees you as someone God could use to serve others is powerful affirmation.

> *I'll never forget the day that God called me into ministry. I decided I wasn't going to tell my wife. I figured it was just too weird. And so I didn't tell anybody for a week—it was the worst week of my life. So finally I told my pastor. Of course he didn't think it was crazy. He said, "You need to tell Becky." So I went home and I said, "I think God is calling us into the ministry." And she said, "You know, today in Sunday school they asked the question, 'If God asked you to move, would you be willing to move?'" And she answered, "Yes." And three months later we moved 400 miles away to go to college. It's the encouragement that I receive from her that I think has really helped me in my ministry.*
>
> —A youth pastor

2. Support by Listening and Offering Perspective

One major way spouses assist and support associate staff members is by being a sounding board, listening to the joys and sorrows, frustrations and jubilations, problems and opportunities of their ministry experiences. Just having someone to listen and be concerned for you and your ministry helps.

> *Next to coming to God himself, my wife is my sounding board. I can come home and tell her everything and anything, and she's always an encouragement. We pray together about it.*

She'll keep me focused on what I need to be doing to remedy the situation. She will offer suggestions, even though sometimes they are ones that I don't want to hear. I don't know how I could do the ministry without my wife.

—A minister of Christian education

When I come home totally discouraged over some thing or situation, he is always able to bring my perspective around. He has just been God's tool. He is able to bring my perspective back around to see it broader rather than this one situation that I think is going to kill me. You know, he helps me to see it so much broader. And his line is always, "The Lord called you into this. You didn't make a mistake. So let's you and I learn to work this thing out." That has been tremendous.

—A director of Christian education

3. Support by Encouraging

When associate staff members are discouraged, having a spouse who can offer words of encouragement can help them shake off the self-doubts and frustrations they carry. Sometimes we are so down that we've lost a proper perspective on who we are and what God is doing.

My husband is my biggest cheerleader and would not let me quit. You know, when I come home and say I want to pack it in, he says, "No. You know those are your gifts, and that's where the Lord wants you to be." He believes in me when I don't even believe in myself.

—A children's ministry director

4. Support through Personal Care

Spouses can be a support to associate staff members by helping them care for themselves and get the rest they need, and by fostering an intimate, caring relationship together. As couples grow to know each other over the years, they can help identify when the other needs time for rest or "re-creation." Many associate staff members appreciate how their spouses help by caring for them and encouraging their spiritual growth.

> *My wife and I have been married for six years, but before that we actually were in ministry together doing youth rallies and things. So she knows me so well that I don't have to tell her what happened. She can kind of read me and by the mood that I come home in she knows what to do. She can either go in the room and start praying for me or give me time just to sit and debrief, or keep the kids away from me so I can think about things. She knows me and reads me like a book and helps me through it.*
>
> —A youth pastor

5. Support by Praying

Many associate staff members look to their spouses as their number-one prayer supporter. Being able to share and pray with your spouse, having her or him bring your personal and ministry needs to God, is a strong source of encouragement.

> *I share with my wife about what's happening in my ministry, and she prays with me at night and for me during the day when I'm at work. It really means a lot to know she's praying for me and the situations I face.*
>
> —A minister of Christian education

6. Support by Critiquing

Sometimes a spouse is a support by being an honest, loving critic. Hearing criticism is not fun, but it can be a stimulus to improvement. When we know that the one who is critiquing our work loves us, and has our best in mind, it can make it a little easier to hear. In the long run, we and our ministries benefit.

> *My wife is one of my greatest critics, whether I want it or not. You know, a lot of times when I don't want it, it's probably*

when I need it most. She'll say, "What was that?" And it's good, because she looks at it through the perspective of just a person who isn't a musician, sitting out in the congregation. She is very honest with me.

—A music minister

7. Support by Hospitality

Sometimes an associate staff member's spouse is a support by allowing him or her to open their home and invite people in with whom they are ministering. This exercise of the "gift of hospitality" provides opportunities to enrich relationships and build a sense of being a team in ministry. Patty helped me host a Christmas open house for all our Christian education volunteers each year. It was a lot of work, but a wonderful time of fellowship.

I couldn't do what I do without the help of my wife. She is supporting me, encouraging me, rooting for me, and then she is practically involved in a lot of things where she is strong and I'm weak. You know, she is excellent in planning the social events. The fellowship, the camaraderie, the fun that happens. And then the choir and the worship team come over on Saturday nights. So a lot of the relationships that have developed over the years have been because of her influence. And my children have all these aunts and uncles, you know, that have adopted them. We've got this sense of extended family because of my kids. It's a blessing.

—A minister of music

The Ministry of Your Children

One striking finding of this study on what helps people thrive in associate staff ministry is the number of ways that their own children minister to them and make ministry more rewarding by their attitudes and actions. For associate staff with children, here is another opportunity for supportive relationships for ministry.

I know that for me there were times when I viewed parenting as an added responsibility and source of stress on top of all that I faced in my position at the church. It was easy to use up all my energy at work and come home grumpy, or seeking a nice quiet haven of rest instead of the homework problems, arguments, and insistent inquiries as to when we were going to go to the park to play. It's easy to fall into the trap of seeing our children as just another drain on our energy instead of as ministers God has put into our lives to help support and renew us. There were times, however, when I recognized what a blessing my children were to me, and how God used them to encourage and support me in ministry.

This support from those we as parents care for comes in many forms. As thriving associate staff members reflected on ways that their children were an encouragement to them, they described four types of ministry they received from their children.

1. The Ministry of Unconditional Love

When my own kids were young, and I returned home each day from working at the church, I often received a hero's welcome. It's funny, but when I showed up at the church office each day I didn't have people run out to greet me, give me hugs and kisses, and tell me they were so glad I was there. But when I went home, I was warmly received by people who were just glad I was me, and that I was home. Other associate staff share similar stories of the unconditional love they receive from their children, and how it helps them weather the stresses of ministry.

> *My family has been my joy and strength, like when the day has gone rotten and your youth meeting was the worst one you ever had. I have two little kids, and every time I walk through the door they go, "Daddy, Daddy, Daddy!" And they love me. And they don't expect me to entertain them or anything. They just want me to sit down and they want to climb in my lap.*

> —A youth pastor

2. The Ministry of Escape

Another way that our children minister to us is by providing another role and aspect to our lives. We are not just associate staff members; we are also parents. There may be frustrations, problems, and stresses in some aspect of our ministry responsibility, but at home we are moms or dads. Switching from minister to parent can be stressful if the needs at home are great, or it can be refreshing, if it allows us to escape the constancy of work pressures.

I open my door and my kids run and say, "Dad, let's play basketball!" Learning how to forget your job is important. If I can forget my job when I close the door to my office and go home, I can be a dad now. I've got the next three hours to play with my kids and then I've got to go to another meeting. I love to play with my kids and just forget about it.
—A children's pastor

3. The Ministry of Help and Understanding

At times our children can provide practical assistance to us as we work to fulfill our ministry responsibilities. Even young children can offer help with little projects, helping to carry our load. As associate staff members see their own children's help and involvement in ministry, it is an encouragement to them to continue in their own ministry.

Sometimes I've had to take curriculum home to prepare for teachers, which is quite an elaborate thing, and they have gone around the dinner table with me after dinner talking about things and sorted curriculum. I recently got remarried, and my daughter pretty literally took over the organization of preparation for VBS [vacation Bible school] and helped me sort things. When the kids were little, they used to come along and sleep in sleeping bags on the floor. It's been a big help to know that they've been very supportive of my work.
—A children's pastor

When I started, my children were younger, but now as they have gotten older, they have really gotten into children's ministries. All three of them are very capable in helping. My 13-year-old daughter could take a class and teach it as well as an adult, so it's been a good training time. But they've also really picked up a real servant attitude. They will come into my office on Sunday morning after they've been to worship and Sunday school, and say, "Mom, do you need help during the 11:00 service anywhere?" You know, they have the option of going home with their father, but it's just really given them a servant attitude because they've seen it modeled. And that's joyful for my heart.

—A children's ministry director

4. The Ministry of Support

When our own children express confidence in our calling to serve and a willingness to support us as we follow God's direction that is a powerful source of encouragement. If we feel that our ministry decisions are hurting our children in any way, it becomes more stressful and difficult to determine how God is leading. Sometimes we can help our children understand more about the ministry God has called us to and seek their help in deciding how as a family we will deal with the new demands we face.

I have an 18-year-old and a 15-year-old, and their thoughts are not always the same as mine, but at least they are support- ive. They can sense that this is what God wants me to do with my life. And so consequently, they are going to go with it. Even my 15-year-old right now, with all her relationships in high school, she believes that if God wants us to move, then we need to move and she would be willing to do that. She says, "Oh, I can make new friends somewhere else."

—An associate pastor

With my kids, as they were growing up, the reason they were supportive is we used to sit down at our family council around the table, and they would decide how many nights Mom could have out. How many hours I could work at the church. Well, because we did that, then they were behind me in whatever I did. It wasn't, "Oh, yeah, Mom is gone again." And so when I would need a little help from them, it worked well.

—A director of Christian education

Threats to Healthy Family Life

Every vocation has its unique impact on family life. Doctors, firefighters, schoolteachers, real estate agents, and church staff members—all have aspects of their work that affect how their families live. For people who serve on church staffs, several aspects of their work and roles can pose a threat to healthy family life. Here are some of the major areas of struggle.

1. Time and Schedule Demands

To some degree, associate staff members in a large church may have a better situation than most solo pastors. While solo pastors are "on call" 24 hours a day, associate staff members may find some relief from this kind of unrelenting schedule. Still, most staff positions carry heavy time demands, often resulting in part-time staff working full-time hours, and full-time staff working 50 or more hours a week. In addition to the time demands, the fluctuating schedule of long evening meetings and weekend activities can make regular time with family difficult to maintain. Six to seven nights out at meetings each week for several weeks place a strain on relationships within the family. Spouses and children may end up feeling neglected, in competition with the associate staff member's work at the church. If this pattern continues, bitterness toward the church and ministry can result, along with damaged emotional ties within the family.

2. Emotionally Draining Work

Along with heavy time demands and an erratic schedule, the very nature of some associate staff roles makes ministry an emotionally draining experience. Even work that we love can be draining. Sometimes we live with the frustration of disappointing results. At other times, we are drained from difficult interactions with people we've been working with. At still other times, we're just tired because we've been working long and hard. If associate staff members use up their emotional resources in their ministries and have scant reserves left when they go home, their families can suffer the consequences. Preoccupation, short tempers, emotional withdrawal, lack of energy for anything except watching television—all are ways we end up robbing our families of their spouse, father, or mother. If this pattern continues over time, it can further damage the quality of relationships within the family and the emotional well-being of all its members.

3. Unrealistic Congregational Expectations

Again, associate staff members in larger churches may find that their experience is better than that of solo pastors. However, most associate staff members find that because of their church staff position, congregations place both spoken and unspoken expectations on their families. A married couple may feel the need to maintain the image of a perfect marriage, even when they are wrestling with serious problems. Their children may feel expected to act more mature than they are, to know the Bible better than other children, to be involved in every church program for kids their age, always to be well-groomed, and to "act nice." Spouses may feel pressure to "have it all together," and to take on ministry responsibilities outside the range of their gifts and interests. Both the associate staff member and spouse may find it difficult to know how to handle and express negative emotions, especially in public settings.

4. Goldfish Bowl Experience

Related to congregational expectations and compounding the problem is the sense of public awareness of one's family life. Because of their contacts with so many members of the congregation and their public roles in church leadership, many associate staff members feel as if they are under constant scrutiny. Everything they do, whether good or bad, easily becomes public knowledge within the congregation. For example, when Patty was pregnant with our first child, she quickly grew tired of people asking her week after week when the baby was due and how she was feeling, offering her advice on what she should and should not be doing, and greeting her on Sunday mornings with "Are you still here?"

5. Awkwardness of Social Life

The high expectations they feel and the inability to escape the role of pastoral staff can make it difficult for some ministerial couples to have a normal social life. This may be less a problem in larger churches, but some associate staff find it difficult to make close friends with whom they can relate normally and not feel obliged to maintain a façade of perfection. Over time, this awkward situation can be discouraging to pastoral couples.

6. Lack of Self/Family Care

One issue that people in vocational ministry must deal with is the tendency to focus on serving and meeting the needs of others rather than paying enough attention to self-care. This orientation is common across the helping professions, contributing to a relatively high level of burnout. The danger for associate staff members is getting so involved in ministry to others that they do not take adequate time for their own physical, emotional, and spiritual nurture. This same pattern can show up in a lack of proper care for their family members. It is like the shoemaker's children having no shoes. He is so busy making shoes for others that he never gets around to making them for his own children. Some associate staff can be so busy working with other people's children, or other families, that they end up neglecting their own.

Strengthening the Home Front

Every family has to learn to cope with the demands that the occupations of the parents place on family life. In spite of the struggles listed above, associate staff members and their families can find ways to foster healthy, supportive relationships together. Here are some specific ways that associate staff members can diminish threats to healthy family life and help themselves and their spouses and children thrive.

Protecting Time for Family

Although there may be seasonal demands that take associate staff members away from their families for a time, ways must be found to keep this absence from becoming a pattern that interferes with strong family relationships. Here are some strategies that others have found helpful.

    1. *Ask for flexible scheduling.* See if your church would allow you to

take some time off during the day if you have a series of evening meetings that week. Take a break and come home when your kids get home from school if you have to go back after dinner for a meeting. Take time out from your day to attend your children's school and community activities. A lot of parents do not have the freedom to do so. It can be a nice "perk" of ministry.

2. *Schedule date nights.* Plan regular times out with your spouse and put them on the calendar. Don't let them get scheduled over. If on occasion you have a conflict, reschedule; don't cancel. If money is tight, even an evening's walk and a cup of tea together is wonderful. It's not so much what you do that counts, but the fact that you do it together.

3. *Schedule family nights.* Same as date nights: Let your children help plan the dates and activities you will enjoy together, and don't let them get cancelled. On occasion, you may have to talk with your family about the need to reschedule a family night, but make sure it happens on the new date. Again, if money is tight, just making popcorn and playing a board game together can be fun.

4. *Learning to delegate and delay.* Strive to keep your schedule from getting overwhelmed. You may need to get your supervisor's help in determining what you really need to be doing, what can be done by others in the church, and what can wait until a future time when your schedule opens up. Also learn to delay nonessential meetings if they are interrupting scheduled family time. I was playing a board game one Sunday afternoon when I received a call from a man in the church who wanted to discuss some theological issues related to a Sunday school class I was teaching. I told him I would be glad to talk later in the week; I was playing with my children right now. He was a bit taken aback and offended that I did not want to drop everything and discuss spiritual things with him. But the fact that the interruption is a spiritual matter does not mean it is more important than time with my children.

5. *Pursue ministry together.* If they are interested, try to find ways you can include your children and spouse in some of your ministry responsibilities. This arrangement can provide you with time to talk and listen to your family members as you serve others together. I have taught or helped with children's church programs in two churches in recent years. My two older children wanted to join me, so they helped with puppet shows, stories, and crafts. Planning and serving together were great and gave them a taste for ministry to others.

6. *Take time off and get away.* Schedule your days off in advance and use them to get away from the concerns of ministry. You may find that you

actually need to get away from your house, or from town, to put it all behind you and enjoy your time together. Resist the temptation to slip back for an evening meeting. Make it a real "Sabbath" day of rest. Don't just do chores all day!

7. *Get an answering machine.* An answering machine (or voice mail) can be used to take messages from others at times when you are busy or out with your family. It can also be used to set up a "hotline" to leave a message for others who may call about church activity details. This investment can save you from answering the phone several times in an evening. (It's also good for discouraging telemarketers!)

8. *Have a daily meal together.* Taking time each day to sit and talk with your family over a meal is a helpful way to stay connected with your children and spouse. If dinner doesn't work, breakfast might. Sometimes everyone in the family is so busy that it's almost impossible to pull this off, but it is worth the effort, even if it means coming home from work a little earlier than usual, or getting up in the morning 15 minutes earlier than normal.

9. *Listen to your spouse and children.* Pay attention to how your spouse and children are feeling about your work schedule. Listen to their comments, and take their feelings seriously. They need to know that they are important to you, even if you still have to go out tonight. Try to find ways to respond to their needs, such as scheduling special times together, getting permission to miss an upcoming meeting, or getting some time off during the day when you would normally be at the office.

> *I definitely have to watch the amount of meetings and other things I take on, because I need to have more time with the kids and family, like helping with homework and other things. I definitely keep an eye on that. When the kids say, "Are you having another meeting tonight?" then I know maybe it's too much. I think the church basically understands. We try to make adjustments if we have a lot of evening meetings; then we take off some time during the day.*
> —A minister of Christian education

Managing Stress and Saving Energy for Your Family

Sometimes, even though we have time available to spend with our families, we're too tired, worn out, or stressed out to enjoy it. As a result, they don't enjoy it either. All we want to do is crash and have a nice long break from having to do anything with or for anybody. If you find that is happening to you, you may want to look at better ways to reduce or cope with the stress you face.

For associate staff members, along with the usual sources of stress in life, there are several aspects of work that can become "high-stress traps." These include:

- Ongoing volunteer recruitment difficulties.
- Too heavy a workload for the position.
- Insufficient salary and benefits to support a family.
- Heavy work demands, making family time difficult to find.
- Unresolved conflicts with the supervising pastor or other staff members.
- Lack of adequate supportive relationships.
- Frequent interruptions from telephone callers and drop-in visitors.
- A change of supervising pastor.

These and other sources of stress can tax one's ability to cope.

The symptoms of too much stress are several:

- *Physical symptoms* (e.g., indigestion or heartburn, headaches, frequent illness, excessive fatigue, chest pain).
- *Psychological symptoms* (e.g., anxiety, depression, irritation, boredom, feelings of hopelessness or guilt, thoughts of running away or suicide).
- *Behavioral symptoms* (e.g., loss of appetite, withdrawal from people, sleeping more or less than usual, difficulty concentrating, loss of interest in or distracting preoccupation with sex).
- *Spiritual symptoms* (e.g., feeling that God is distant, difficulty maintaining accustomed spiritual disciplines, withdrawal from fellowship or groups, feeling dry, "going through the motions" in worship or prayer).

If these symptoms are beginning to show up in your life, take them as a sign that you really are not doing well, and that you need to make changes.

Three basic approaches can help you learn to cope with your stress holistically.[1] We all employ some of these approaches some of the time, but when our stress loads go up, we have to learn to expand our coping styles and take better care of ourselves.

1. *Reducing your sources of stress.* Some of your stress may be self-imposed. Your self-expectations may be too high, driving you to tackle more than you should. Your interpretation of your life situation may be skewed, causing you to feel victimized or helpless to change anything. In these cases a change of perspective can help reduce the stress you feel. It may be helpful to seek out a good counselor who can help you reflect on your self-expectations and life perspective and adjust them to help you reduce your stress. Other practical steps that can reduce sources of stress include:

* Setting goals and priorities to help you determine what to take on and what should wait for later or be handed off to someone else.
* Addressing and resolving conflict situations instead of hiding from them and allowing them to fester.
* Strengthening your time-management practices and scheduling.
* Reducing overcommitments if possible through delegation, postponing, or getting help from others.
* Seeking counsel from others who can help you deal with your problem areas.

2. *Coping with unavoidable stress.* Since you cannot get rid of all the stress, develop good coping methods to help you face and work through it. Several helpful approaches include:

* Keeping an open communication with God about your life situation through prayer and worship, seeking divine wisdom and strength.
* Seeking out social support from a friend, talking through your issues with someone who cares for you.
* Taking up enjoyable physical activities, reducing the effects of stress on your body, taking your mind off stress, and freeing up some endorphins (chemicals in the brain) to help you feel better.
* Mental diversion through entertainment, concerts, reading.
* Taking up a hobby or personal interest outside your work, like gardening, crafts, or sports.
* Taking mini-vacations or "Sabbaths" away from your work.

3. *Building your health to handle stress better.* Finally, you can strengthen your capacity to handle stress through taking good care of yourself. Adequate sleep, good nutrition, regular aerobic exercise, and spiritual disciplines that feed and strengthen you—all will help you cope better with the stress of life and ministry. Don't wait until you are "stressed out." Take care of yourself, and seek God's strength in anticipation of the work demands you know will come.

Dealing with Congregational Expectations

There is no way to escape totally the congregation's expectations of you and your family, but when those expectations are inappropriate or unhelpful, you can minimize their impact. For example, if you feel the pressure of having to display a perfect marriage and family at all times, you may need to develop friendships outside the congregation to give you the freedom to be more open about the ups and downs of family life and to escape the feeling that you are always being watched. If your spouse feels pressure to be involved in certain ministries in the church, he or she may need to take initiative early to identify his or her gifts for ministry and where they fit best, and then get involved in those areas. If your children feel they are expected always to be role models and on their best behavior, you may need to intervene on their behalf and help others understand that your children are no "holier" than others just because they are part of a staff member's family.

> *A Sunday school teacher had to put my daughter in the corner because she was acting up. And that's good; I need her to be disciplined because she has ADHD [attention deficit hyperactivity disorder], and she needs to be dealt with at times. And the teacher kept going on and said, "We do expect more of our staff's children." And I went, "Wait a minute. I don't want you to expect one thing less from her, but don't you ever expect one thing more. She is a child, a human being. Don't do that." The lady was just stunned. My daughter doesn't get my paycheck at the end of the month, and she didn't necessarily get my calling. And I pray to God that she'll have the call to be a child of God, but not a youth minister's daughter. She never filled out the application for that.*
>
> —A youth pastor

Building a Richer Social Life

Even though we may enjoy spending time with church staff and members and having time at home with our families, this limited range of friendships may not be enough for us or our spouses. The demands of work and family responsibilities may make it difficult to develop meaningful friendships with others. However, part of what helps people thrive in ministry is the range of supportive relationships they have developed and their ability to escape the stresses of life temporarily. Having an active social life can be good therapy for us and our relationships with our spouses. Ways to do this abound, and we all have our own interests and opportunities. Let this list of ideas stimulate your own thinking.

- Join a community sports league and get out to play once a week or more (e.g., softball, bowling, basketball, volleyball, curling).
- Get tickets to the community theater and invite friends to go with you.
- Set aside two nights a month to invite a family over for dinner and board games.
- Go to local college or professional sports events with friends.
- Volunteer in a community-service organization, and invite others in the group to go out for coffee when your work is done.
- Set up a "supper-six" and take turns once a month hosting dinners in your homes.
- Throw seasonal parties, and look for excuses to celebrate life's special events with others (e.g., Thanksgiving, Christmas, New Year's Eve, Easter).
- Get others to join you in skating, bowling, going to the beach, skiing, boating, fishing, walking, or some other favorite activity.

The important thing is to plan ahead for these kinds of social gatherings and make them a regular part of your life. Just how frequently you do this, and how many people you want to spend time with, will depend on your and your spouse's personalities and interests.

Balance: Time for Personal and Family Care

One danger of a clear and strong call to ministry is that in our minds it can overshadow the other responsibilities God calls us to fulfill, including loving and caring for our family members and taking proper care of ourselves. We can become consumed with doing our ministry well and end up neglecting those closest to us. One long-term minister of music described his own struggles and insights:

> *I was probably a workaholic until my second child came along. The first child was pretty much left to my wife. I wasn't that interested in little babies anyway. The second child came along and was a child that didn't sleep, and my wife basically shut down. So I had to really rethink every aspect of life and ministry. I had some good mentors and role models on the staff at the church that helped me through that. Getting permission to do less around the church, even permission to do less than the congregation expected, not just less than I expected, was something I had to learn to do. That was a very good time, and I've been able to maintain some pretty healthy balance since then. When I see other music pastors getting into trouble because they're workaholics, it's just one more reminder that I don't have to do more than what God wants me to do. And one of the things God wants me to do is take care of my family. I'm the only dad my kids have. I'm the only husband my wife has.*

Along with everything else said in this chapter, it is important that associate staff members who want to thrive in ministry over the long haul learn how to find an appropriate balance in their lives between the ministry and their care for their families and themselves. Many suggestions have been offered for taking time with your family and friends and for your own renewal. Make a commitment to spend time with your family on a regular basis and a commitment to your spouse and to God to nurture your own spiritual growth and emotional health. Let God give you a life that is full, not just busy.

> *Survival is not forgetting that you do have a home that needs to be nurtured along with your concern for your other family, the "church family" that you have. You are responsible for that home, also for a wife or husband, whichever it might be, and also for those children that are there. A lot of times it's said the deacon's children are the best children, because the*

minister of youth is with them all the time. And the minister of youth's children are rotten, because he is not able to be with his own kids. So it does go back to balance, and also appreciating, respecting, valuing that family that you have of your own, because they give you the best support.

—A music minister

Take Care in How You Dump

Finally, while a spouse and children can offer great encouragement and support when we're feeling discouraged or frustrated with conditions at the church or in our ministries, we must be careful how we share our frustrations with them. Because they love us, they may quickly come to our defense and grow angry with others in the church. It can be helpful to unload frustrations on a good friend first, letting off some of the emotional steam that has built up. Then it may be appropriate to share with your spouse, discuss the frustration together, and pray together about it. Later, be sure to tell your spouse how the problem is resolved, and rejoice together when things go well. Several associate staff also warned against talking about frustrations and conflicts with their children, cautioning that it can too easily sow seeds of resentment and bitterness toward the church.

One reason why I don't share with my wife first is because she defends me to a fault. A half-hour conversation with her and I am convinced that they are all jerks. These other guys will tell me I'm a jerk sometimes. My wife, God bless her, she's so wonderful to me, she just defends me to a fault. I think that is a wonderful support, but you need the balance of perspective too.

—A youth pastor

Sometimes I have come home and caught myself griping and bringing up things that happened to me, and it started embittering my son and daughter against the church. "How dare they do that to you, Dad? You've done so much. I'm sick of this junk. They're a bunch of jerks. Why didn't you stay working for Pepsi, Dad? They treated you better." They don't need to hear any of this stuff. So maybe you should be honest, but I don't think that honesty does our children any good. I don't want to plant any seeds Satan can use for bitterness in my children. I want them to be in the church. I blew it, so I'm telling you from my mistakes. Be careful. Don't bring it to your kids; don't bring it up. I don't think it helps them.

—A youth pastor

For the Single Associate Staff Member

For associate staff members who are single and childless, this chapter may seem either irrelevant or discouraging. It may seem irrelevant because it deals with relationships with one's spouse and children, which the single staff member does not have. It may seem discouraging because it highlights the ways families minister to married staff members, while the single staff member may long for that same kind of support and encouragement. Even though this chapter is focused on married staff, unmarried associate staff members can find and nurture the same kinds of "family" relationships to support them in ministry.

It is important to note that being single in ministry is both exemplified and encouraged in Scripture. Jesus himself never married, and Paul was single as he carried out his ministry as portrayed in Acts and in his epistles. Paul encourages others who are able to remain single to do so, focusing their efforts on serving God (1 Cor. 7). Those who serve while single suffer no disadvantage in God's eyes and in fact may find it easier to follow God's call to ministry.

All associate staff members, whether married or single, benefit from developing supportive relationships with people outside their families. This need is evident in Paul's own letters as he greets and speaks fondly of those who have served with him and with whom he has shared fellowship. Single associate staff members may want to focus their efforts on nurturing supportive relationships. If a single person wishes to go further and to develop more family-like relationships, one can find ways to develop such friendships that can enrich one's life.

Sharing a house or apartment with friends, having supportive roommates to spend time with, talk with, and care for, can be an encouraging experience. If you live a distance from your parents, finding an older couple in your church or neighborhood with whom you can spend time and talk to as surrogate parents or grandparents can be of great support, and may be a blessing to them as well. Finding a family in your church who will adopt you as a "cousin," "uncle," or "aunt" can bring rich relationships as you relate to them as brother and sister and to their children as they grow. Forming close friendships with other singles in the church, enjoying activities, meals, and ministry together, can be enriching to all concerned. Opportunities abound for loving, caring relationships to be built and close long-term friendships to be formed. Make the development of these kinds of supportive relationships a priority in your life and ministry.

Taking Inventory: Questions for Reflection and Discussion

As you reflect on your family situation, the threats to healthy family life you face, and the things that you have already done to strengthen your family relationships, take some time to work through the questions that follow, either on your own or with someone else. Some questions to discuss with your spouse and your children are also included. Take time to gain their perspective; it may give you new insight on what is needed and how to respond.

Questions for You to Consider

1. Is your ongoing work schedule so demanding that you have little regular time with your family? Do you have time to spend talking with them, doing things together you all enjoy? If time is a problem, what options might your church consider to reduce the negative impact of your crowded schedule (e.g., flexible scheduling, regular days off, delegation of responsibilities)?

2. Are your ministry demands so stressful or emotionally draining that the quality of the time you have with your family is affected? How are you coping with stress? From the stress-management section of this chapter, what could you begin doing that might help you better manage stress, freeing you to be a more enjoyable and supportive family member?

3. Do you feel (or do you think your family feels) pressure to have your family conform to some unrealistic, stressful congregational expectations? If you do, it may be helpful for you to discuss this issue with someone else, such as an older pastoral couple whom you respect, to sort through your feelings, discern how you are reading the congregation, and generate ways you might respond.

4. Are you feeling a lack of privacy as a family, as though you are always under scrutiny by others? Is this attention making it difficult for you to work through family problems or disagreements? If so, can you carve out times to get away from the church and community as a family and develop a greater sense of normal life?

5. Are you or your spouse feeling unable to make the kinds of close friendships and enjoy the kind of social life together that you would like? What opportunities are there in your congregation and community for you to get together with others with common interests? How can you make time in your schedule for such fellowship?

6. Do you feel that you have lost a sense of balance in fulfilling the roles and responsibilities God has given you in your family and work? What areas are suffering? What do you think is needed to restore that balance? What help do you need? How and where will you start?

Possible Questions for Discussion with Your Spouse

1. What do you like and not like about my being a church staff member? How do you think my ministry is affecting us and our family?

2. What kinds of stress or expectations do you feel because of my ministry responsibilities? How might I help you in reducing or coping with them?

3. Has my schedule over the past few months provided adequate time for us to spend together as a family? What do you wish we could do that we have not been able to do recently?

4. When I am at home, do I seem preoccupied or stressed out to the point that it interferes with our relationships as a family?

5. How can I show my support and love for you better?

Possible Questions for Discussion with Your Children

1. What do you like and not like about my being a church staff member? How does what I do affect you?

2. How do you feel about the kind of work schedule I have to keep? What do you wish we could do that we have not been able to do recently?

3. Do you feel that my work makes me grumpy with you?

---

1. These recommendations for coping with stress are adapted from Walter H. Gmelch, *Coping with Faculty Stress* (Sage Publications, 1993); and from Gwen S. Faulkner and Terry D. Anderson, *Stress Indicator and Health Planner* (Consulting Resources Group, 1990).

CHAPTER 8

Savoring Joys and Weathering Storms

> *Let us not lose heart in doing good, for in due time we will reap if we do not grow weary* (Gal. 6:9).

For people in associate staff positions, regardless of their ministry responsibilities, few things are as satisfying and motivating as seeing positive results in the lives of those to whom they minister. Seeing that their ministry is bearing fruit in the lives of others confirms their calling and assures them that God is able to use their gifts and efforts. It is also rewarding to see that what they value and have given their lives to achieve is coming about. This realization is the source of their greatest joys in ministry.

However, associate staff work is never an unbroken string of ministry successes. Positive results are not always easy to see. Problems arise from various sources, making ministry difficult. Some ministry efforts seem to fail, discouraging the associate staff members who have invested themselves so heavily in them. Many look for new positions in other churches, or even leave vocational ministry altogether, because of discouragement in the face of ministry storms.

Those associate staff who have thrived in ministry over the years report that they have learned to do two things well. First, they have learned to rejoice in their ministry successes and savor them, allowing them to be a source of encouragement, satisfaction, and motivation to continue in the face of difficulties. Second, they have learned to handle tough times and deal with discouragement, criticism, and conflicts. This chapter looks at these two areas, providing practical ideas for savoring the joys and weathering the storms of ministry.

Sources of Joy in Ministry

Sharon has served as a children's pastor in her church for almost 15 years. She has given and received more hugs, wiped more noses, and talked with more parents than she can remember. Each year, there are challenges, some bigger than others. Recruiting and training volunteers, planning Christmas events and vacation Bible school, meeting with teachers and program leaders, finding replacement teachers on Sunday morning—these tasks can eventually take it out of you. There have been many times over the years, especially lately, when Sharon has felt worn down, just plain tired. When crises hit at times like that, she can feel discouraged. She sometimes wonders if she should resign and turn the position over to someone else. When this mood hits, she does two things to lift her spirits and renew her energy for ministry. First, she makes sure that she gets to spend time with the children, talking with them, exchanging hugs, enjoying their presence. At her church, punch is served to the children every Sunday, so she heads over to the table and starts pouring punch and talking with the kids. Second, she pulls out her "fuzzies file" and looks at pictures and reads cards and notes written to her by children and parents over the years. God uses these two things to restore her joy in ministry and allow her to savor it.

Joys in ministry come in many shapes and forms and from many sources. When thriving associate staff were asked about their sources of joy in ministry, they cited these kinds of experiences.

Children's Pastors

When you walk into a room of children and they recognize you and stop crying.

Watching children you worked with grow up and graduate from high school.

Some of the children I had 20 years ago are now grown, and some of those are involved in ministry, and that makes me motivated. It's really exciting whenever you go to the altar to pray and one of those 20-year-olds comes up to pray and to affirm what you are doing, as well as what they are doing. That's a real breathtaking thing now.

Going into a grocery store and suddenly hearing, "Debbie, Debbie, Debbie!" I turn around, and there is a van full of kids that come to our midweek program, bus kids. Out comes a mom I've never met, and I'm charged. That's a great moment, because I know there is a whole family potential now, and we've been trying to get to that.

Seeing a child make a commitment, and then watching them and seeing a change, and having a parent confirm it. That keeps me going a really long time.

Watching adults who come in with fear and trembling to be an assistant, and three years later they are running a whole department and they've found their niche, and they say to you, "Thank you for asking me to teach." That is cool!

The thing that brings me joy is when something works really well and I see the workers have joy working with the children.

Youth Pastors

For me, it's seeing kids become either volunteers or professional workers in the church as adults now. I don't think there's anything that gives me more joy.

The greatest thing is to somehow have confirmation back from the Lord that what you're doing is valuable, what you do matters, what you have done through the power of the Holy Spirit has increased the Kingdom or made a difference in it. To be able to hold onto that is just the best.

Just seeing any progress in my kids at all! You've got your kids who are new to the group and they'll invite another friend, and that means a lot. And then you've got your person who is involved in youth ministry, but then they take steps to do deeper Bible study, or they graduate and come back after a couple of years and they want to be on staff with you. Everyone is at

*different points, and if you can just monitor any type of pro-
gression, it means the Lord is blessing and being merciful. I'll
go for that!*

*It's pure joy to me when you remember this twerpy little teen-
ager you just wanted to smack, one of the kind that just caused
nothing but grief, and you invested a lot of time, energy, and
prayer over. And you're at a national youth gathering, and
this handsome adult walks up who is there with his five adult
sponsors and 35 kids. And he says, "I wouldn't be here if it
wasn't for you." That's joy!*

Directors/Ministers of Christian Education

*I get pleasure in seeing somebody benefit from a discipleship
group or a small group that I got started, something that they
feel really helped them.*

*Seeing people actually responding. Maybe on the basis of the
teaching or training you have done, you actually see them
become more productive. I think that is really gratifying, because that's what we are all about. Getting people equipped
and actually seeing that person serve more effectively.*

*I've learned to really focus on my areas of giftedness. When I
do that, I find a lot more joy in ministry than if I allow myself
to be sucked into all the administrative details that are very
draining for me.*

*I just happen to have some kids in my college group now whose
parents were in my college group a long time ago. Seeing that
come back around is a blessing.*

*This almost feels selfish, to see a young man or woman accept
Christ and to see the light come on spiritually. Just to be around
it, you might not have had anything to do with it, but just to be
around and witness that. I can't put it into words—it's better*

than a million dollars. To know that you have a purpose in life that transcends making a buck, gaining respect, whatever ambitions you have. It makes up for the paychecks that aren't what you'd be making if you were teaching or whatever.

Music/Worship Ministers

I'm one of the most blessed people in the world because I have been able to take my two greatest loves, my love for the Lord and my love for music, and put them together, and that's my job. God has called me to help people really experience his presence in worship. Last Sunday, we were singing, and a lady in the front row had a tear come into her eye. I asked her after the service, "What happened in the service this morning?" She said, "I was so full of the presence of God I couldn't even sing anymore." Some of the greatest joys of music ministry is to be able to see people really experience the presence of God.

My job is to equip people to do the work of ministry. And so whenever we see people succeed and get to the point where they can be ministers and are equipped to do that, that is very rewarding. People coming to know Christ and then being built up and equipped to do ministry, and then doing it.

A woman came to see me about her husband, who had problems singing, and she said, "See what you can do with Lawrence. He just can't carry a tune. He's just so embarrassing to me." Poor Lawrence was standing there, you know, six feet, two inches, this big old guy. And I worked with Lawrence briefly. Then on Father's Day, there was Lawrence and his four sons in the Father-Son Choir. His face was just absolutely radiant. That's another moment of pure joy. It's just the times that you invest in people. When you see those seeds grow, it's such a blessing.

Associate Pastors

My joy comes out of seeing the joy in other people's lives. They discover who Christ is, and whether they become a teacher or discover a spiritual gift or ministry, they get involved in serving others. I think that's where my joy is, in seeing them being able to do that and find some sort of wholeness or completeness in that.

I'm behind a desk all week planning the ministry, but on Sundays I make a point of being at the punch table, serving those little cups of punch to the kids, and I'm talking to them and saying "Hi" to them. And my joy is when they come up and I feel those hugs around my legs, and they say, "Thanks for the birthday card." Or, "Guess what I did? I caught a fish this weekend." Those little things remind me why I'm here and what I'm doing.

Committee meetings are usually boring, but every once in a while when you see a committee look at a need or look at a possibility of a ministry and take a courageous step, whether it's money or what they are going to do to get out in front of an issue. Whether it's a need to be met or an opportunity to be taken, they are going to press forward, and it's not the staff. They are going to do it together. They're going to be right alongside you. Boy, when that happens, it's the "ah-ha" moment. You know, we've grabbed this purpose together somehow. It's gotten out of the theology books and the Scriptures, and it's now living here in this group.

Reading over these types of comments, one sees a few common threads concerning joy in ministry for associate staff members.

First, some joys take time to develop. Some of the fruits of our labors are not readily evident, but if we stay at it long enough, joy can come as we see how God works in the lives of those we have served.

Second, joy comes not just through our own ministries, but also as those we have recruited, trained, and supported become fruitful in ministry.

Much of our joy of ministry is "vicarious joy" as we see others in our ministry areas exercise their gifts.

Third, joy comes in our interaction with the people we serve, not in higher attendance numbers or higher levels of giving. It is change in the lives of people that brings joy. When people come to faith in Christ, grow to know God better, and follow in obedience in their daily lives, that is rewarding.

Fourth, joy comes when we see ministry come full circle, when those to whom we have ministered grow to the point that they begin to minister to others. This kind of "ministry multiplication" is deeply satisfying.

Finally, joy comes when we see that God has taken our gifts and passions for ministry and by grace has used them to make a difference in the Kingdom.

Savoring Ministry Joys

Since some of the joys of ministry can be fleeting experiences, thriving associate staff members have found ways to "capture the moment" and allow it to become a source of encouragement when their circumstances are not as pleasant. They intentionally find ways to remind themselves of the joys and successes of ministry during times of discouragement. Here are a few things they have found helpful that you may want to consider doing as well.

The "Joy File"

Many associate staff members have put together a file or box where they place thank-you notes, letters of encouragement, and other mementos of ministry highlights. When they begin to grow tired or discouraged in ministry, they open up that file or box and read through the contents, taking time to remember how God has worked in the past. This material becomes a source of encouragement as they face the demands of the present.

> *I have this Tupperware box thing that I can't even put a lid on that I keep encouragement letters in. When I've had bad days, I'd reach in, "Man, where's that one note, where's that letter? Ahhh, OK." I know that sounds bad, because we should be*

getting our joy from the Lord, but still, that's where I was at.
Now I can get a note and just stuff it in there, read it later, and
go, "Thanks God."

—A youth pastor

I find if someone writes something and gives it to me, that
means so much. Lots of people say nice things, but just hav-
ing something in writing enables me to savor what God is
doing in and through me, and gives me something to read at
times when I'm discouraged.

—A director of Christian education

I have a "fuzzies file." I keep it in the front of my file drawer,
in my desk. It's notes of encouragement that I've gotten from
people, thank-you notes, cute little drawings from kids that I
end up with. Sometimes I kind of journal on a piece of paper
and throw it in there. When I get really discouraged and think,
"Oh, it's going really bad," I pull it out and look through it
and say, "There is joy in this."

—A children's pastor

The Picture Board

Because so much of the joy of ministry is related in some way to the people
we serve, many associate staff members have found that keeping visual
reminders handy of those they serve and work with is another way to remember what the ministry is all about, why it is important, and how God is
working through them in the lives of others. Whether it is a photo album, a
bulletin board of pictures and other mementos, or pictures drawn by children put on the office door, these visual reminders can be sources of encouragement and motivation in ministry.

Leading kids to Christ—I don't know anything that even comes
close to matching it for joy. Probably the second place would
be as I pass them on to the subsequent years in high school
to see them faithfully serving and to see them be an integral
part of the next program up. That's important. And the way I

preserve it, I never take down kids' pictures. Our youth room is littered with pictures of people who used to be there too, because it's a constant reminder of praying for those kids and seeing where they are at.

—A director of Christian education

I have a drawer full of knickknacks from kids I have had in my youth group. Every now and then I'll open it up and paw through them. It can make me a little sad because I miss them, but it's a great encouragement as I think back on all we did together and how they have grown.

—A youth pastor

Anniversary Collections

For some associate staff who have served in the same church for a number of years, having an anniversary celebration with a chance to collect letters or notes of appreciation from the congregation is a meaningful way to reflect back on ministry accomplishments and to be encouraged to remember the joys of ministry. This may be an awkward thing for associate staff members to initiate. But if they have a committee they work with closely, the group might be prompted to action by an expression of how meaningful this kind of milestone marker would be. I know that when I had served in a church for five years, the Christian education board held a surprise picnic in my honor, and it was a wonderful time of celebration. What a lift to one's spirits! Having a photo album of notes and pictures from that kind of event can be a wonderful reminder of God's grace in ministry.

Our greatest joys come in long tenures where we have seen growth and we've been able to watch teenagers grow up, go off to college, marry, have their own baby, and been able to share with them all along the way. On our 15th anniversary, the church put together a compilation of notes from the people. We periodically go back and read those notes. They are a great source of joy.

—An associate pastor

As you think about the tangible reminders cited above, ask yourself what kind would be meaningful to you and help you savor the joys of your ministry.

Weathering the Storms of Ministry

Learning to savor the joys of ministry is important in part because other times come for all of us when life and ministry become difficult. Instead of clear sailing, we find ourselves swamped by stormy waves of ministry or personal problems. For some associate staff members, these storms are so overwhelming that they end up looking for a new church to serve or a new vocation. Quitting may be a necessary response in some situations, and those who leave should not be judged for not "hanging in there." God works with each of us differently and is able to "cause all things to work together for good to those who love God, to those who are called according to His purpose" (Rom. 8:28). We need to focus on our own ministry situations and how we can best weather the difficulties we will face with perseverance in following God's direction in ministry.

Long-term associate staff who are thriving in their ministries have not had all clear sailing. They too have experienced ministry and personal storms that could have taken them out of vocational ministry. In the midst of their difficulties, by God's grace, they found ways to weather the storms and persevere until the tumult passed. Their reflections on how they weathered storms revealed concrete steps that you may want to work through in your difficult situations.

1. Seeking God's Guidance and Help

The first response to ministry difficulties is to talk to and listen to God, humbly seeking divine guidance. It is an acknowledgment that full knowledge and wisdom reside in God, and that I may be ignorant, blind, and even wrong in things I have done or how I perceive the situation. My only hope for making it through this present difficulty resides in God's guidance and grace.

I always go back and ask the Lord, "What am I to learn through this?" as opposed to "These are the problems and these are

*the people that are frustrating me." That's been good, be-
cause I think we always need to be humbled. You know, we
are not always right, and we are in a growing process. We
haven't arrived.*

—A children's pastor

This kind of humble spirit before God is critical for learning and growing in ministry. I may have made mistakes, or I may lack the wisdom to deal
with the current situation, but I serve a God in whom all wisdom resides
(James 1:5-8). If I open myself up to God's instruction, through the means
and people God provides, I can learn, grow, and become a better servant
leader in the church.

Some of the approaches to this kind of prayer that have been helpful to
thriving associate staff members include:

Mini-retreat. For some people, getting time away in a "mini-retreat" is
helpful. This activity has already been discussed in some detail in chapter 5.
Having the opportunity to get away from the situation, even from the people
involved, can help staff members gain new perspective. This time away
with God can help heal emotional hurts and reduce defensiveness so they
can hear what God may want to teach them.

*There are times when I just have to be away from everyone,
times when I am so wounded I need to be away from people.
This gives me time and distance to heal.*

—A director of Christian education

*Sometimes I have to take the afternoon off and say, "You know,
I can't do any more. I'm not working any good for anybody.
Lord, I need time with you. I'm going home, or to the park."*

—A children's pastor

Keeping a Journal. Some associate staff find that taking time to write
their thoughts and concerns in the form of a journal or letter to God is
beneficial. It helps them sort through their feelings, bring their needs and
concerns directly to God, and open their hearts to hear what God may want
to say to them.

I journal. I share my frustrations with God, releasing the con-trol back over to him. Usually by the time I shut the journal I feel like it's God's battle, and I'll let him change things that he needs to change, and even change my heart if he needs to change my heart. That's probably the biggest help for me with my frustrations.

—A women's ministry staff member

Prayer at the Altar. Our own sanctuaries can be places of retreat for periods of prayer. Even though we know that God hears us wherever we pray, praying in the sanctuary can sometimes help us focus our thoughts. We are reminded of God's presence as we have worshipped there in the past. Praying there also serves as a reminder of those we serve, and our obligation to bring their needs to God as well.

There is a spot down there; I might as well have knee pads. There is a spot in front of the altar that's mine. My knees fit there very comfortably. And I do a lot of praying.

—An associate pastor

2. Revisiting Your Calling and God's Guidance

When ministry storms hit, they often cause us to question our ability to serve, even whether we should be in ministry. During these times of chal-lenge, it can be helpful to take time to revisit our calling by God to serve in vocational ministry and to recall how we have been directed and provided for in the past. One long-term associate staff member commented that he was able to weather ministry storms in the present because he had already seen how God had helped him weather them in the past. For new associate staff, our first big storms scare us into thinking that we can't survive them, that we need to abandon ship. But our veteran associate staff colleagues are able to put current problems into perspective because they have seen and remember how God has worked before.

Taking time to remember God's grace and provision in the past can give hope and confidence in the present. We still need to seek God's direc-tion for the present, but we need not be ruled by fear that we will not be able to handle the demands we face. God is able to strengthen and guide us if we are to persevere where we are. We need to remember that the ministry is not ours, but God's.

> *I was reading in the Gospel of John this morning, and the first verse I read was "Let not your hearts be troubled. If you believe in God, believe also in me." The last verse I read was "Remember, greater is he that is in you than he that is in the world." I think when I get most frustrated, I have to remember whose job it is, and who the ministry really belongs to, and almost take myself out and then analyze the situation. And that helps give a little more perspective to it and brings it back to reality.*

—A children's pastor

3. Seeking Support from Others

While being alone with God is helpful for restoring perspective and gaining direction, God has also provided us with people who can support us through the ministry difficulties we face. Scripture instructs us to bear one another's burdens (Gal. 6:2), encourage one another and build each other up (1 Thess. 5:11), pray for one another (James 5:16), and stimulate one another to love and good deeds (Heb. 10:24). God knows that we gain great encouragement from the ministry of others in our lives, and it does not signal a lack of spirituality to turn to others for support when we find our ministry demands overwhelming.

Chapter 6 addresses the variety of supportive relationships that associate staff members can develop to help them thrive in ministry. When we face problems in ministry, these people become a safe haven for talking through our feelings and concerns, gaining wise counsel and personal support, being held accountable for our actions, and being encouraged and prayed for. They complement rather than replace the ministry of the Holy Spirit in guiding and supporting us. The richest people in associate staff ministry are those who have both an open, intimate relationship with their Lord and Saviour and the loving support of their brothers and sisters as they serve the family of God.

4. Coping with Stress

Even while we seek God's counsel and direction in prayer, review our calling and God's provision in ministry, and seek the support of others as we face our ministry problems, we need to address the impact that ministry problems can have on us personally. Ministry storms dump a load of stress on us, taking a toll emotionally, physically, and spiritually. As we take action to reduce the causes of stress, we also need to cope with the stress we feel. Chapter 7 has a fuller section dealing with ways of coping with stress in ministry. Read it over, and look for ways you can better cope with the stress you feel. As long-term associate staff reflected on actions that helped them weather ministry storms, they highlighted a few ways of dealing with stress. Read these over and consider what you find to be most helpful in relieving the stress in your life and ministry.

> *If it's just stress because I'm not handling things well, sometimes I just need to voice it. I've got people that I can go to, to let off steam, leave it on their desk, and walk away. If it's stress because I don't have enough hours in the day, I know I can go to my supervisor and get help.*
>
> —A children's pastor

> *Having a hot tub helps a lot.*
>
> —A children's pastor

> *I go to the gym and work out, play my violin, listen to Scripture tapes and Scripture music.*
>
> —A children's pastor

> *I have a couple of praise tapes that I put in, and I just praise God.*
>
> —A children's pastor

> *Sometimes just a good cry doesn't hurt at all.*
>
> —A children's pastor

> *You have to be real intentional about having fun! I've started taking country-western dance lessons this year. That's something I've wanted to do all my life. When things are getting*

stressful, I go out and dance, and it's a great mind relief. I just really, really enjoy that, and I can laugh, and play, and have fun. And then the next day I can come back and look at it again and have a fresh perspective.

—A director of Christian education

I have gotten to the point of writing names on golf balls and hitting them at the driving range. Somebody caught me doing that one time, and now I have a golf ball on my shelf in my office with somebody's picture on it. They actually went and got pictures and had them put on some golf balls. I nearly died, so now I hide it.

—A youth pastor

I don't see my work as eight-to-five. I see it more in terms of seasons. Some seasons, like vacation Bible school or things like that, you just know they are going to have an all-out press to get everything done. But I try to reward myself after. I plan for a time that I can look forward to and say, this is going to be really hard work for this length of time, but after that, then I'm going to do these things with my family or for myself.

—A children's pastor

Finally, don't forget that God is able to relieve the stress we feel as we pray and receive the peace offered through the Holy Spirit.

Be anxious for nothing, but in everything by prayer and sup-plication with thanksgiving let your requests be made known to God. And the peace of God, which surpasses all compre-hension, will guard your hearts and minds in Christ Jesus (Phil. 4:6-7).

Taking Inventory: Questions for Reflection and Discussion

As you consider the ups and downs of ministry and how you are responding to your current ministry situation, it may be helpful to work through these questions, either on your own or with your spouse or a colleague. This can be an opportunity for you to encourage and support each other in savoring the joys and weathering the storms of ministry.

Savoring Joy in Ministry

1. When you think about your own joys in ministry, what things come to mind? Are you so focused on the stresses and problems of ministry that you are not seeing the ministry successes that could be an encouragement to you and increase your joy?

2. Do you have a "joy file" or box where you keep notes, pictures, and other mementos of your ministry? If you do, when is the last time you looked through it and took time to give thanks and praise for God's grace and goodness in your ministry? If not, why not start one now and look for things to put into it that can be reminders of ministry successes and joys? How could you use this file or box during times when you are struggling in ministry?

3. Do you have a picture board, or some other way of displaying pictures and mementos of people and positive ministry experiences? If not, would having such a display be a helpful visual reminder of why God has called you to serve here and the people who have been brought into your life and ministry?

4. Do you have a ministry anniversary milestone coming up that would be a good occasion to celebrate? How can you take initiative to do this, and to whom else could you turn who might help with the celebration? What would make it meaningful to you?

Weathering Ministry Storms

1. When you face stresses and problems in your ministry, is your first reaction to grit your teeth and work harder, or are you taking time to pray for God's guidance, peace, and strength? How much are you consciously turning to God for help in your ministry, and how much seems to be on your own effort?

2. Would taking time out for a mini-retreat help you gain perspective and strength for the ministry challenges you face? Can you get permission to do this? Are you getting adequate time for quiet prayer? If not, what needs to change to allow you this time?

3. When was the last time you reflected back over how God has called, equipped, and guided you in ministry? With whom can you share your story who would encourage you as you deal with ministry pressures? Would writing your story out like a journal entry be helpful in reviewing what God has done to strengthen and guide you?

4. When you are under pressure in ministry, do you tend to isolate yourself, withdrawing from others who could be an encouragement and help to you? Who are the people you can turn to for support as you face ministry pressures and struggles? Do you need to take initiative in developing more supportive relationships, connecting with others, and supporting them in ministry as well? Reread chapter 6 for more ideas on how you can strengthen this area of your life and ministry.

5. When ministry storms hit, how do you cope with the stress you feel? Do you have activities to relieve your stress? Are you using them? What else could you do that might help in managing the stress of ministry? Reread chapter 7 for more ideas on how you can increase your ability to cope with stress.

CHAPTER 9

Thriving Skills for Female Associate Staff

A gracious woman attains honor (Prov. 11:16a).

Because I lack the experience of being a woman associate staff member, being able to sit and talk with women who have served as associate staff members for years and who are thriving in their ministries was a helpful learning experience. In addition to the focus groups with women associate staff, women made up almost 30 percent of the veteran survey respondents, showing that many are indeed thriving in their ministries, not just surviving.

This finding is encouraging, since women have historically had a more difficult situation to deal with in vocational ministry. Previous studies of women in associate staff positions have highlighted a number of factors that make thriving in ministry a harder goal to attain.

First, opportunities for women to serve on church staffs are often more restricted for both cultural and theological reasons. Some churches or denominations limit women staff to certain ministry areas, such as women's or children's ministry. Since many associate staff positions include a broader range of pastoral responsibilities, some churches prefer a man for these types of positions. This can make locating an associate staff position more difficult for women than for men.

Second, job titles and ordination opportunities offered to women may not reflect the full pastoral status available to male staff members. Some churches and denominations use the title "director" for women staff and "pastor" or "minister" for male staff members. Some also reserve ordination, or even licensing, for men. This practice may reflect the more limited ministry responsibilities these women staff carry, with ordination and the title of pastor granted only to those who carry a broader pastoral role. It may also reflect a theological or cultural hesitancy to identify women officially as pastors. In other cases it may be the result of reserving ordination and the title "minister" or "pastor" for those who have earned a master of divinity degree; some women associate staff members do not have an M.Div. Whatever the reason, job titles are one way of conveying status in the Christian community, and ordination or licensing can also provide some tax benefits that may not be available to many women staff.

Third, women occupy more of the part-time staff positions than do men. For some women, serving part time can be a good way to stay involved vocationally in ministry while caring for the needs of their families. However, part-time positions have limited pay, and the work-hour demands frequently exceed the job description and pay received.

Fourth, more women than men in associate staff positions are single. While spouse and family support is beneficial in enabling associate staff members to thrive in ministry, single associates lack that type of immediate, constant family support. In addition, single women may receive lower pay than their male counterparts; with no spouse to bring in additional income, a woman may find it difficult to survive financially.

As a result of such factors, women may find associate staff ministry a relatively easy field to enter, but a more difficult one to thrive in over time. The fact that so many female associate staff members are thriving shows that by God's grace, these obstacles are not insurmountable. God helps women associate staff not only to survive the demands of ministry, but also to thrive and find satisfaction and fulfillment in it as well. Along with the items described in earlier chapters of this book, which apply to men and to women alike, it is helpful to look at those factors that are especially important for women to be able to thrive in ministry.

Thriving Factors for Women Associate Staff

The difference between male and female associate staff members is not so much which factors are important to each, but that many of the key factors are even more important for women. These "more important" factors can be grouped into four areas: the importance of flexible work schedules, supportive networks, continuing education, and personal spiritual growth.

1. A Flexible Work Schedule

Among the realities facing many women in associate staff ministry are the competing demands of caring for family and fulfilling ministry obligations. Whether caring for preschoolers or older children after school gets out, responding to the needs of older parents, or fitting in with a husband's work and vacation schedule, many women staff value having some flexibility in their work schedule to allow them to respond to these kinds of needs. When a church is able to provide the flexibility needed, the stress facing a woman associate staff member is reduced, helping her find more satisfaction and joy in fulfilling these diverse life roles. Even women whose children are grown value having flexibility in their schedule to spend time with their adult children and their grandchildren. The critical issues are to reduce the stress of conflicting demands and to maintain a balance in life among roles and responsibilities. (While men are not exempt from the demands of family life, it is more acceptable in our culture for a man to focus his efforts on his work and to rely on his wife to respond to immediate, daily family needs. In families where both husband and wife work, men may feel these tensions more than if the wife were not employed outside the home. The need for flexibility in the work schedule may grow as a concern for male associate staff as well.)

If you recognize that you face tension in fulfilling your roles in your family and at your church, you may want to explore with your supervisor or board ways that you can adjust your schedule to relieve some of that tension. Some possibilities include adjusting work hours to be home when your children are out of school, restricting the number of evenings you have to be out each week, doing some of your work from home, and having school holidays off. There may even be times when you would value a leave of absence (e.g., pregnancy or maternity leave), or temporarily cutting the position back from full time to part time (e.g., caring for an ailing parent, summer schedule when children are out of school) to free you to fulfill the family roles you value. Take the initiative to explore these kinds of possibilities to help you reduce stress and enjoy your ministry more.

2. A Strong Support Network

Because of the issues they have historically faced in ministry and the tension of competing demands from family and work roles, women associate staff members especially benefit from a strong network of supportive relationships. These relationships form a source of strength, companionship, and encouragement to carry out their ministry responsibilities. It may also be true that women in general are more relationally oriented, valuing a network of relationships for its own sake more than men do. Whether or not this is true, the importance of a strong support network is expressed in how women associate staff identify the value and influence of four types of supportive relationships for their ability to thrive in ministry.

Supervisor. First, the role of the supervising pastor as an encourager and cheerleader is very important. Because some people may question the legitimacy or ability of women in ministry leadership roles, the visible, consistent support of the supervising pastor is necessary for building credibility in ministry. It is important that a woman associate staff member have the full support of her supervising pastor and feel encouraged to exercise her gifts in ministry. Women staff also report that having a supervisor who affirms them when they are discouraged, and who encourages their professional, personal, and spiritual growth has been a powerful influence in their ability to thrive in ministry. Three women made clear just how critical this kind of support from their senior pastors was for them.

> *You need a supervisor who believes in you more than you believe in yourself. That's all the more important for women for longevity. For me, being a woman has actually been a positive thing. Doors have opened for me. I think the senior pastors I have served under were glad I was a woman, and would rather have had a female in that position than a male. Being a woman has actually broadened my life, but I think that is probably still an exception.*

> *A key thing for me has been a strong senior pastor who supported and protected me, was willing to stand up for me, and willing to take on people on my behalf. I was ordained at my church, which had never ordained a woman before. Until years later I didn't realize that the pastor put his entire ministry, career, life, and reputation on the line for me. I'll tell you, that's an encouragement to stay in an associate ministry position when you have that kind of a senior pastor.*

*When I came on, I really didn't know what I was getting into.
But my pastor interviewed me and said, "Whatever you do, I
want you to know I'm 100 percent behind you. And whatever
comes up, or whatever problems you have with parents or
teachers, I'll back you all the way." To know ahead of time
that somebody is behind you all the way is just great encouragement. It gets lonely on that limb.*

Support Group. Second, regular participation in an accountability or
support group of peers in ministry is highly valued. Because the experience
of women in ministry is somewhat different from that of men, and there
may be more ministry stresses to cope with, it is important that you find
other women in ministry with whom you can talk. Having the opportunity to
discuss ministry issues with people who truly understand you, you can gain
encouragement and wise counsel from each other. If you are on staff in a
community without any other women associates, you may need to make
contact with others across the county or state and arrange times to get
together. This type of gathering has enough benefit to it that it would be
good to gain permission from your supervisor to put it in your work schedule
on a regular basis. One woman told how her group functions.

*I have a support group of women in different areas of minis-
try. We meet weekly, and we're networking with other women
in professional ministry in our area. We find support and encouragement amongst each other from parachurch and church
ministries—lots of support.*

Prayer Partners. Third, having one or more prayer partners has a
significant impact on female staff members' ability to thrive in ministry.
Because of the stresses and challenges of ministry, it is important that you
have people you can turn to who will pray for you, asking that God would
give you wisdom, grace, and strength to carry out your ministry. Women
associate staff members rate prayer partners as a very strong influence on
their ability to thrive in ministry. They can be members of your support or
accountability group, members of your church, or members of your family.
In fact, in many cases it is other women in the congregation whom the
woman staff member looks up to as people of spiritual maturity. Some women
find it beneficial to have one or two close prayer partners with whom they

share deeply, and many others who help pray for their ministry needs in more general ways. However you do it, find people who can intercede for you and your ministry, supporting you as you serve.

Mentors. Fourth, a mentor—another woman who has traveled the ministry road, to turn to for counsel, encouragement, and as a model—is a valuable resource. Having someone you respect in ministry from whom you can learn and draw encouragement can be of tremendous help, especially during times when you question whether you can meet the challenges you face. In survey results women, more than men, reported that this type of mentoring relationship was significant for their ministry. Two women related how their mentors helped them.

> *There are a couple of women in ministry that are older than me that I watch. You know, I just watch their lives and I watch how they deal with obstacles and how they deal with being a woman in ministry in a man's world. And when difficult things come, I watch their responses and then I watch God honor that. So when I come to those obstacles, you know, I choose to look at them, because they are also women that make different decisions and their lives are harder. I've gone to them and shared with them, "You know, I watch you, and your decisions mean a lot to me."*

> *I have gotten to know some women who teach in a college and seminary. They mentored and discipled me. I think probably the thing that has helped me most in longevity in ministry is their attitude as women in ministry. Neither one of them had a chip on her shoulder and their attitude was, "God has called me. He has called me to give the best that I can, gifts, abilities, the talents, the training that he has given me. That's all he has called me to do. He has not called me to fight battles, he has not called me to any of that other junk." And that has kept me in ministry without a lot of the battles and scars that I've seen in other people who have gone out there angry. God would have never been able to use me as much had I gone out swinging.*

3. Continuing Education

Over 90 percent of both male and female thriving associate staff members attend professional conferences, conventions, or other educational events for continuing education and for networking with others in their area of ministry. Women report that such events are a very influential factor in their ability to thrive in ministry over the years. This rating may be due in part to differences in education between some men and women associate staff members. Continuing-education events may help some women address ministry issues that they have not previously had the chance to study. It may also reflect the value of these settings for women as a place to make contact with other women in ministry and to develop supportive networks that extend beyond the educational event. Whatever the reasons, the experience of women associates is that these kinds of continuing-education events are a source of help in their ministries, improving their ability to thrive. It may be helpful for you to look actively for continuing-education events in your ministry area and to submit a request to your supervisor and church board for the time and financial support to attend. Try to make this a regular part of your ministry schedule, and use these events not only to gain knowledge and skills for ministry, but also to connect with others in ministry and to strengthen your network of supportive relationships.

4. Personal Spiritual Growth

While similar percentages of men and women associate staff members have spiritual disciplines that strengthen their faith and their relationship with God, women more than men report that this practice is influential in their ability to thrive in ministry. Women also value, more than men do, having their supervisor encourage their spiritual growth and well-being. In general, more women than men report the practice and value of extended times away in prayer (retreats). While more men report the practice of regular Bible study for personal growth, more women than men rate it as influential in their ability to thrive in ministry. The reasons for these differences are not clear. The survey results may reflect the impact of a more stressful ministry setting for women and a heightened awareness of the need for God's strength and guidance, but there is no hard evidence to back up this hypothesis. The findings may also reinforce a perception of women as more spiritually attuned, valuing the meditative practices of prayer and retreats more than men do. Again, the reason is not clear.

Whatever the explanation for this difference, it seems important for women associate staff members to develop and engage regularly in spiritual disciplines that nurture their spiritual vitality and growth, treating this practice as integral to their ministries, not just an exercise done when there is free time. How are you keeping such disciplines in the midst of your family and ministry demands? Which disciplines are most beneficial to your spiritual vitality? Are you shortchanging your own spiritual health in the name of ministry productivity? Spiritual growth must become a priority for your long-term health and well-being in ministry.

Advice on Thriving from Veteran Female Staff

When veteran women associate staff who love their ministries were asked what advice they would give to women starting out in associate staff ministry, the overwhelming focus of their comments was on the necessity of patience and grace as a woman functioning in a man's ministry world. While they addressed the importance of an encouraging, supportive supervisor, the value of a support network, continuing education, flexibility in work schedule, and personal spiritual nurture, most of their comments addressed how to proceed in ministry with patience and grace. Being a woman in associate staff ministry is not an easy thing, but with these two qualities it can be rewarding and fruitful. To thrive over the years requires a measure of each. Here are veteran women's comments and recommendations.

> *We have to be women and not try to be men in our positions. We don't have to act like a man, trying to take a man's way or approach. For longevity, you have to do a very, very, very quality job. You have to be better than average if you want to stay the long haul as a woman in a position in ministry. And you have to be willing to know that everything you do is judged. What you do as a woman in ministry, because you're probably one of very few that people will be exposed to, will affect all other women in ministry. So I think as a woman in ministry you have to serve with a sense of responsibility. My greatest frustrations have been women who, because of how they fought*

their battles, because of their bad attitudes, have made it more difficult for me. It's not fair, but it's reality.

The reason I didn't want to be in children's ministry was because that's what women did. And I had to work through the issues of what society and the world say about women and that whole thing. And I said, "Lord, I just want to be used by you." And I learned to walk in that submittedness to the Lord. He opens the doors and sense of calling following that. When I came into this position, I had to be very wise about how I did things. I just stayed really low-key for a long time until I proved myself, and that I had earned the right to be heard. Now I have a wonderful relationship with the senior pastor and the senior executives who respect me and listen to me. When I speak, they listen, and they respect that. But it has taken me six years of just allowing God to do that because of things I had inherited or things that had happened in that situation to the people before I arrived. And God has redeemed all that.

Be satisfied in your role and accept your role or limitations without a fight. Move gently towards change. If you go out for a fight, I don't think you are going to get very far. I find that if I move gently and I'm assured of myself in the way that I live, I get much further than if I go out for a fight.

There are four of us women on our staff of about 22 pastors. I've really appreciated the sensitivity of the men. When they came back from a conference (they all went and we four women didn't), they were talking about the "walls coming down." And I remember one of the guys I was sitting next to at staff meeting looked at me and said, "How are you feeling with all this?" And I said, "Well, I think there are some walls that haven't come down." I didn't say it smart. And later we were praying, and he prayed for us women, and the sensitivity the men need, and sometimes the comments that are made, that they haven't treated us well, you know. And I really appreciated that. Yet I'm in a church where I'm not considered a pastor. I'm a director, and sometimes that bugs me.

We have had women on our women's ministry board who would get angry about this and that, and I mean the concern has been justified, but they've fought their way. I want to portray another image of what women are like. That you can sit in a meeting and strongly disagree with the men you are working with, but say it in such a way that it doesn't become an emotional issue, or is said in such a way that you lose ground for yourself, as well as for the women you work with.

Encourage the men you work with. We want to be encouraged, but I think we need to encourage and affirm them, what they do in their work, as well as the other staff [nonpastoral]. We also need to pray, and pray, and pray.

Taking Inventory: Questions for Reflection and Discussion

Each woman's ministry situation is different. Some feel tremendous support for what they are doing and have many people to turn to for encouragement and counsel. Others feel more isolated in their ministry roles with few supporters and encouragers. It is important that you assess your own ministry situation and needs and take steps to develop the supportive resources and practices that can help sustain you in ministry over the years. Read over the following questions and take time to respond to them, either personally or in discussion with someone who knows you and your ministry situation well.

1. *Schedule flexibility.* As you look at family and work roles, do you feel conflict over whether you can meet competing demands? Would you benefit from some adjustments to your work schedule? Are these kinds of adjustments possible, or do you have to stay with the current situation? Whom would you need to talk with to see what kinds of helpful changes could be possible?

2. *Supervisor support.* As you look at your support network, is your work relationship with your supervisor such that you feel supported and encouraged in your ministry? If you think the support may be there, but it is not being communicated to you well, how could you raise the issue with your supervisor and share the kinds of expressions of sup-

port that would be meaningful to you? If this kind of support is not forthcoming, whom else can you turn to for this kind of encouragement?

3. *Support group.* Are there other women in ministry you can meet with regularly to discuss ministry issues, share needs, and pray for each other? If you are not aware of any nearby, what organizations could you contact (e.g., denominational, community, professional organizations) that could help you locate other women in ministry? What would you most appreciate from meeting and talking with this kind of group?

4. *Prayer partners.* Do you have one or more people with whom you are able to be open about your personal and ministry needs and who will pray with you and for you? If not, what women do you know in your church or community whom you respect for their spiritual maturity and with whom you could begin to develop this kind of relationship? Whom could you partner with for mutual prayer support?

5. *Mentors.* Do you have contact with other women with ministry experience whom you respect? Even if they are not nearby, how could you begin to talk with them and learn from them? Are there some women who have been models to you in the past but with whom you have lost contact? Perhaps you could take the initiative to reestablish contact and talk with them about what you have learned from them in the past, and how you would like to be able to talk about personal and ministry issues with them if they are willing.

6. *Continuing education.* Are you taking advantage of professional training events (i.e., conferences, conventions, courses, workshops) in your ministry area at least once a year? What opportunities do you have that you have not pursued? If you are afraid that the expense is too high for the church to approve, but you have an event that you think would be beneficial for you, can you talk with your supervisor about it and discuss possible sources of support? Are you committed to continuing to learn and grow in your ministry skills? If so, how are you living out this decision?

7. *Personal spiritual growth.* What spiritual disciplines have been most helpful to your faith and spiritual vitality? What kinds of helpful

practices tend to get crowded out by your busy ministry schedule? How can you carve out the time to pursue them? Reread chapter 5 for more ideas of what might be helpful to try.

8. *Grace and patience.* Do you find it difficult to exercise grace and patience in your ministry position? What kinds of things most frustrate you? Have you found ways to begin to address these frustrations so that those in leadership will listen to you and understand your views? Do you have supportive people who are able to hear your frustrations and to provide support and counsel in how to respond to them? Are you making these frustrations the focus of prayer for wisdom and grace so that you may give positive, constructive leadership in your ministry?

CHAPTER 10

Veterans' Advice to "Wanna-bes" and "Newbies"

> *I remind you to kindle afresh the gift of God which is in you through the laying on of my hands. For God has not given us a spirit of timidity, but of power and love and discipline* (2 Tim. 1:6, 7).

One of the joys of conducting research for three years with hundreds of thriving associate staff members has been listening to them share their own experiences, telling how God's grace has enabled them to find joy in ministry, despite the difficulties they have faced. I always closed the focus groups and surveys by asking participants what advice they would give to new associate staff members about what new staff can do to thrive in ministry over the long haul. The advice covers a wide range of issues, often mirroring the issues addressed in the preceding chapters. It seems appropriate, in concluding this section of the book, to allow the many study participants to speak for themselves, offering their counsel to "wanna-be" associate staff and "newbies." The quotations that follow come from all kinds of associate staff members (e.g., differing in gender, ethnicity, ministry responsibilities, denominational affiliation, full-time and part-time, U.S. and Canadian). Listen to your brothers and sisters in ministry and ask God to help you identify issues that you need to address in your life and ministry and those things for which you can give thanks and praise. May God give you insight to strengthen and equip you for fruitful and satisfying ministry.

Calling and Commitment to Your Ministry

- Have a sense of God's call on your life for specialized ministry, because there will be times when the need for your ministry will be questioned (especially in a time of financial crises).

- Consider the call! What task has God called you to? Too often we jump at a position or ministry opportunity because it fits our dream. Is it our desire (lust) or God's call? If it's our desire, when troubles come—we're gone! If it's God's plan and his call upon our life, we're serving him, and he gives us the strength to endure until he says time's up. He shows us his purpose and plan for our ministry—whether immediately or eventually.

- Everyone is not "made" to be the number-one guy. There is nothing wrong with being number two (or number three or number four). Know what your gifts are and don't try to do things you are not equipped or gifted at doing.

- You must see your ministry as an associate as an end in itself and not a means to something bigger or better. An associate who sees his position as a stepping-stone will by definition be discontented with his role and that attitude will be reflected in subtle yet discernible ways. People have asked me if I will ever become a "real pastor." I smile and tell them gently that I am a real pastor and I enjoy my ministry very much. I am every bit as much an undershepherd in this ministry as the senior pastor is; we just occupy different roles.

- Commit yourself to staying at a place for a minimum of three years if possible. This gives you time to survive the first-year honeymoon, discouragements, victories, and other battles. This also gives time for you to know the people's hearts and to allow the people to understand your heart, vision, and direction.

- Commit to serve for the long haul. You'll need to be open to God's call elsewhere, but assume it's here until he tells you otherwise.

- Think long term! Much of the fruit of your ministry comes after year five.

Interviewing for a Staff Position

- Interview your future church and senior pastor carefully.

- Be very careful in choosing the church and staff with which you will have to work. There must be a genuine understanding of team ministry, a lack of territorial domain, and a desire to reach goals together.

- Make sure there is a good match between you and [the] church (theology, lifestyle); you and [the] pastor (areas of strengths and weaknesses complement); make sure [the] pastor is a team player.

- Have a clear understanding of the senior pastor's vision, calling and philosophy of ministry. Often it is as much "the will of God" who you work for as where you work (i.e., [the] question is not "Can I work in Toronto?" [The] question is "Can I work with this pastor?"

- Go into the job making sure that your style of ministry is in line with that of the senior pastor and the congregation. Don't try to change your convictions or style to get the job. It won't work for long.

- Be clear about where your "gifts for ministry" will fit into the long-term goals of the congregation.

- Be sure God has called you to be an associate. If not, be honest with your pastor and church about your goals and plans.

- Know yourself (spiritual giftedness, talents, and abilities) and don't try to be someone you are not. Don't become a chameleon for the sake of acquiring a job.

- Get a very clear job description. Especially for a part-time staff person, you need to know exactly what is expected of you.

- Make sure you have a clear job description and annual work reviews.

- If you're married and so is your senior pastor, ask yourself how will your spouses get along. Does the senior pastor's wife's style or presence place your spouse in a bad light? Will they ever become close friends? You can be happy in your slot, but if your wife is miserable, you won't last long.

Relationship with Senior/Supervising Pastor

- Remember that it is our job to make our senior pastor look good. . . . She is still "where the buck stops." We must never contribute to divisiveness, or in any way make our senior pastor look foolish. If we can't follow [her], we need to resign.

- Never, never (unless he is clearly going against Scripture), undermine the senior pastor, even to your [spouse] or friends.

- You are there to protect his back! In return, the senior pastor (hopefully) will guard your back and be your defender as you will defend him.

- If you disagree with the pastor, do it behind closed doors! Always show him respect, but remember that you don't have to lose your own in the process.

- Develop a mutually supportive relationship with the senior pastor. You may need to push for this, but don't let it slide or think it will take care of itself. You need each other, and you need to know you can trust each other.

- Be open to a personal friendship if your superior desires it. If the superior does not initiate it, determine honestly how long you can minister without it. However, don't hold a grudge if the superior does not become a personal friend.

- Before you can expect your own vision to be respected and realized, it is important to learn to share someone else's vision. Simply realize that you are not the primary vision-builder of the church. Find a way to establish your vision within the confines of the senior pastor's vision.

- Accept the fact that some decisions must be made by [the] supervisor—keep in close contact, work to communicate constantly.

- Set your heart on supporting the senior pastor's vision, helping [her] to fulfill [her] mission. When you reach a point that you can no longer support that vision with integrity, then now is time to leave. When you leave, go with strong words of support, no matter what you experience.

- Being a good associate staff member is difficult, but so is being a senior pastor. (I served as interim senior pastor for two years during a vacancy.) Be careful not to deceive yourself into thinking that the grass is greener on the other side.

- You may gain the respect and admiration of many members, but always remember that they want to and will give their greatest respect and devotion to the senior pastor. Accept that fact!

- Be respectfully up-front with [your] senior pastor. This may be difficult if you're young ... and new in ministry while the senior pastor is older and well-seasoned, but candor is essential. Without the trust that flows from open, honest communication, staff relationships will deteriorate and subtle resentments will build. Then it's only a matter of time before the empire falls.

- Don't embarrass your superior publicly. Don't put [her] on the spot to make a decision on the part of your ministry in a staff meeting. If you've got an idea you want to run by your supervisor, do it in private. Let [her] have time to mull it over and think about it. It's very, very crucial that we don't surprise our senior pastor with anything in a staff meeting.

- Remember that your senior pastor can learn from you. You have been called to serve God and his people with the gifts he has given you. Just because you are in an associate position doesn't mean that you are in an inferior position, so learn how to see your senior pastor as a colleague, not just as a boss. There should be mutual accountability. Let your pastor know that the fact that you disagree with him does not mean you are disloyal to him; as partners in ministry you should be able to work through disagreements about philosophy of ministry and other important issues in such a way that you both grow in your effectiveness in serving God and his people.

Important Things to Do as an Associate Staff Member

- Realize you are a team player. It's not your goal to have the best ministry within the church; rather, your goal should be that your church becomes more Christlike. Help the youth pastor when he needs help. Be willing to pitch in your time in other areas of ministry. You're not a Lone Ranger.

- Be a good team member. Work through situations with fellow staff members. Don't let them fester. Compromise if necessary.

- Surround yourself with a lot of good people. Train them and then empower them. Don't feel like you have to do it all yourself, even though you know you can probably do it better than they could. [If] we want our senior pastor to empower us, we have to be willing to empower other people.

- Listen to people who have been there for a long time and who know the heritage of that church, because each church is different. Be sensitive to what's going on and don't try to change everything all at once.

- Build up, encourage, and be fiercely loyal with other staff members. Do not ever talk behind their backs. If you do, it's the beginning of the end.

- Get to know the staff you work with, as well as the senior pastor. Get to know them as a person; try to see their area of ministry through their eyes. Try to see how their ministry fits into the big picture as opposed to being wrapped up in your own world of ministry responsibilities.

- Maintain [a] good working relationship with other associates. The whole team of associates must focus on supporting the senior pastor. At the same time, back up each other because we need each other to survive.

- Don't allow (or do not invite) placing on you professional responsibility in which you were not trained, [do not] have skills, or lack interest.

- Develop relationships with the people. People who love you and view you as a person with integrity will follow and make your ministry dreams happen. People who feel "used" do not follow well.

- In the long haul, you're not going to be effective if your walk with God is not growing and your relationships with people are not positive. You can mess up a whole lot of tasks, but if your relationships with people are right, you're going to be ministering regardless. I think we so often tend to get things backwards. I see a lot of people doing ministry and really botching relationships and that concerns me.

- Maintain an open relationship with a church board member to communicate vision, goals, problems, and prayer.

- Change things in a new church slowly. Maintain what's going on and don't change until you have informed and won over the volunteer leaders and the senior pastor. For genuine change to take place, true long-term change, it's going to take a long time for that to occur.

- Come in with a servant's heart to observe and see what's going on. See what's working. Evaluate what's not and why it is not. Gradually begin to implement. I think if you can earn the trust and the confidence of people, it helps when change is needed.

- Stand up for your rights and your place and your calling, as often folks, mostly innocently, do not understand what an "associate" is. They confuse associate with "assistant." Although it can become totally frustrating, continue to educate those around you, in an easy, low-key, nonstressful manner, who you are and the possibilities you have within you. If you bury the frustrations, they will erupt when least desirable.

- Pray a lot and listen to God. Love and accept God's children and families as created in his image.

- Be quick to admit failures and ask for forgiveness.

- When you [have] grown tired of youth activities, or any type of constant work you once enjoyed, consider moving to another staff position. If you can't find one you like, maybe you should be a senior pastor or leave the ministry altogether. Don't stay in a position for the paycheck. Enjoy your calling or leave. The church doesn't deserve your burnout.

- Understand that any church that has people in it has problems. Don't leave because of problems or frustrations. You are likely to encounter the same ones (or worse) in a new place. Like they say, "Better the devil you know than the devil you don't."

- Learn to endure, to be flexible, to fail. In all things give thanks. It comes with the territory, the good and the bad.

- Respect the tradition that you are coming into. Respect the worship style (ministry style) that has been there and understand the importance it has in the people's lives.

- If, indeed, God has called you, then be genuine and transparent in what you do. Allow people to see your heart. That is one of the ways you are going to reveal God. If you are knowing God, then you can reveal your own heart to people and say, "You know, this is who I am." Allow them to get to know who you are. You don't have to be like someone else. Realize the person you are; that's all you can be.

- Learn two phrases: "Why do you ask?" and "You may be right."

- Trust that God is faithful. If he has called, he will equip, and he will pay your salary or provide for your need. Laugh occasionally; read good joke books.

Checking Your Attitudes

- Be content with your calling. In the church today we cannot all be senior pastors. Being on staff at a larger church provides many more opportunities in ministry than being a solo pastor in a small church.

- The grass isn't always greener on the other side—just ask those grazing over there. Talk to others in ministry; they usually are facing the same frustrations.

- Always remember who you are serving and whom you need to please. God is your final and most ardent supervisor. If you are truly serving him and pleasing him, nothing else really matters.

- Keep Jesus Christ as your focus. It's his body, his church, his work, and he will keep it going.

- Don't fool yourself. Many young ministers are building their own ministries. You are "in" ministry, and you are God's vessel. He is building, and you are but a part of his master plan. You are expendable. Stay focused on the Lord and what he wants to do. Don't be a steeple climber.

- Do not let the foibles and flaws of [the] senior pastor destroy your commitment to ministry and to serving the Lord through your church. Most senior pastors do not understand nor appreciate the ministry and the impact that associate ministers have. Do not let this lack of appreciation influence your service and your commitment. Keep your eyes on obeying the Lord and following Christ.

- Our results don't happen overnight. Some lives are changed many years later. Looking back, I now see where God is using me and has used me in places I didn't see when I first began my ministry. Don't give up on yourself or your kids!

- Don't let ego get in God's way. Dissension among church staff leaders can usually be traced to a power struggle. There is only one power source. Let him be your guide.

- Be flexible, always eager to learn and grow.

- My favorite motto is: "Blessed are the flexible, for they shall not be bent out of shape."

- Always remember God isn't interested in our ability, just our availability to him. He can make us what he wants us to be and teach us all we need to know if we make ourselves available to him first!

- You need to have a certain amount of humor. You must be resilient. That is a critical area you must have.

- Other than a relationship with God, don't take things so seriously. It's going to go wrong—so what? Ease up on yourself.

- Expect disappointments with people, but don't let that get you down. Don't be disillusioned.

- It is also very important to not look at the people for what they can do for you, the position they can fill or something like that, but to have a genuine love and care and concern for them as individuals first.

- Continue to recognize the advantages of being . . . associate staff rather than the senior pastor.

- There is equality in calling, but differentiation in position. This is crucial! Do not view yourself as inadequate or second class as an associate.

- Do not expect credit. You are part of a team, and credit usually goes to the leader.

- Don't expect praise or rewards on this side of heaven. If this happens, fine; but if it doesn't, fine. I've seen a lot of people quit because of discouragement.

Supportive Relationships Outside of Staff

- Find an accountability partner and/or mentor, somebody right from the start that you can confide in and meet weekly with and build into your life as well as use as a sounding board to share your concerns, complaints, struggles.

- Make sure you have at least one person of the same sex who is an accountability partner, before whom you are absolutely transparent. Take time for deep praying with that person. (The accountability and transparency should be mutual.)

- Have others who support your work and affirm your calling to your vocation meet with you on a regular basis.

- Find a support group. Others in staff positions are probably in the same boat! Pray for each other.

- Listen to the criticism of your spouse and significant others.

- Invite feedback and wholesome criticism, "and you will be elected to the wise man's hall of fame" (Prov. 15:31-32 [Living Bible]).

- Develop Christian friendships outside your church—people with whom you can bear your soul and share your struggles.

- Develop relationships with non-Christians. Get out of the church and into the community.

- Mentor new believers.

Taking Care of Your Family

- None of the congregation members are going to move with you when you leave—only your family. Make sure you spend time with them. If your church does not understand your need for time at home, go elsewhere.

- Draw boundaries for your personal and family life and stick to them. Your ministry is never done. There is always more to do. Balance is so very difficult and so very necessary.

- Maintain balance, time for fun, time for self-care. (It's not being selfish). And, most of all, lots of warm, intimate, face-to-face time with your spouse. Without his/her knowing with certainty that he/she is loved more than you love the church, you will crash and burn in time.

- To keep family times as top priority and to "date" as often as you can. A happy home equals a successful ministry.

- I also believe that God called me to be a father and husband, which at times takes priority over my ministry to the church. The family is God's institution and I serve him there! Personal growth is important in understanding work/family relationships.

- Stability (long-term) in ministry is extremely healthy for [spouse and] children.

Leading a Balanced Life

- Strive for balance between work, family, recreation, relationships, etc. Don't become a workaholic. Ministry will eat you alive.

- Always remember [that] you can never get it all done. There will always be something to do, so use good time management while working, and when the day is done, go home and find outlets for personal relaxation to keep yourself fresh.

- Take time for healing, retreats, meditation time, sports/exercise, vacations. Don't come back for funerals, special events, etc. Remember that the church has been here before you and will continue after you. Do your best, but keep your perspective and sleep at night.

- Set boundaries (ministry has a tendency to bleed) especially for time for prayer, Bible study, recreation, and family.

- Make and keep boundaries: get rid of beepers, pagers; keep a "date" night; take your day(s) off.

- Make sure you have regular days off. One day a week is barely adequate—almost sinful if you have a family. At least every second week an additional day should be taken off. On your day off, stay away from the church.

Ongoing Self-Renewal and Education

- Take care of yourself—personal growth, development, physical well-being, emotional, mental health—and don't assume that others will take care of you.

- Make regular appointments for yourself and keep them. Use them for reflection, journaling, planning, dreaming, strategizing and generally going to the "press box" of life to see the big picture.

- Continue to develop your professional gifts/skills, even if not currently using them in the present ministry setting.

- Continue to get input from others or from conferences and seminars. I found mentoring relationships and exposing myself to conferences extremely helpful. Go where you can grow. Get in a ministry that will minister to you as well as allow you to minister.

- Insist on ongoing ministry education and development so that you can expand your thinking and network with others who do things differently.

- Be a self-directed learner. Develop a plan for personal, comprehensive growth. Be a reader. Attend conferences, avail yourself of local opportunities to learn, attach to a peer group of "professionals."

Relationship with God

- Your personal relationship with God is the most important thing for your ministry and your own personal life. As you listened to God's call in the beginning, it will be affirmed to you again by the Lord that you are doing what he wants you to do. This helps more than anything to keep on keeping on. That is your strength. That is the way to take the

Scripture, "I am the way, the truth, and the life" means that to find God's way for your life is in the person of Jesus Christ. Your connectedness to him is your lifeline.

- If you are an extrovert, take time for prayer—not petition or thanksgiving, etc., but for quiet listening to the voice of God within you.

- Prioritize your own personal walk with God. Make sure you're truly meeting with him regularly in devotional Bible study and prayer. Never be satisfied with the "status quo" spiritually.

- Worship—take time to renew yourself and your relationship with God. Often we are so busy worrying about other people's salvation that we neglect our own. Allow time every day to pray. [It] sounds easy, [but is] not always so in associate staff circles.

- Don't always expect the senior pastor to charge your battery. It's unrealistic to expect him [or her] to meet your every spiritual need. Find personal spiritual disciplines and positive peers and mentors to help you stay strong.

- Discover what it is that feeds your soul and replenish regularly. Make it part of your job. You can't minister to others if you're starving yourself.

- Find your worth and your role in Jesus Christ. Don't be dependent upon the pastor or congregation for affirmation, acceptance, and approval. Look to your personal daily walk with God for strength, direction, encouragement, and support.

- Walk in surrender to the Lord. Learn to ride the waves God creates, not create the waves. The wave God creates may come after we take a step of faith, but the only reason the wave was created is because God gave us the reward of our faith. Learning this will maintain a sense of *rest* in God. He only gives strength for his plan.

- Keep your focus on Christ in good and difficult times. Recognize and understand the work of the Holy Spirit. Know your Bible and never stop studying it.

- Stay in touch and in tune with God—don't get so busy that you leave your spiritual life behind. Ministry can be a roadblock to spiritual growth.

- Continually grow deeper in love with God the Father, Christ Jesus, and the Holy Spirit.

AMEN!

For Those Who Care about Associate Staff

Thriving in ministry requires more than the individual effort of the associate staff member. Every associate works with others in a congregational context. Other factors in this context contribute to the associate staff member's longevity and satisfaction in ministry. While this book was written for associate staff, others need to be aware how they can contribute to the well-being of staff as they carry out their ministries. In these appendixes, I address this broader audience of supervisors and church boards. Associate staff members should read this section themselves and then share it with the appropriate people in their ministry setting.

Appendix A is addressed to those who supervise associate staff members. While in most churches this will be the senior pastor, that is not the case in all situations. Whoever it may be, much of how associate staff members feel about their ministries is tied directly or indirectly to their supervisors. While every work relationship develops out of the actions and attitudes of each person involved, supervisors are in a position to have a great impact on the ministry longevity, satisfaction, and personal well-being of their associate staff. Appendix A summarizes what thriving associate staff value about their supervisors and suggests how a supervisor can work with his or her associates to bring these things about. To assist supervisors and associate staff in discussing issues and practices that can enhance their ministry together, permission is given for the duplication of one copy only of this introduction and appendix A for the supervisor to read and use. Questions are provided at the end of the appendix for reflection and for discussion with those supervised.

Because so many work-setting factors can affect an associate staff member's ability to thrive in ministry, appendix B was written for the oversight body of the local church that deals most directly with the work of church staff. Churches of different denominations have various governance structures and processes, so no attempt is made to specify who needs to do what. Instead, issues and general principles are presented to assist those who have the responsibility of overseeing the needs and work settings of associate staff members in their church. Permission is given to make one copy only of this introduction and appendix B for each member of the relevant church board or committee. Questions for reflection and discussion are provided at the end of the appendix.

It is my hope that through reading and discussing the issues and principles raised, associate staff, their supervisors, and lay leaders will find increasing effectiveness and joy in ministry together. Working well together in ministry multiplies joys and relieves the burden of stress. May God enable you to experience that kind of relationship in ministry together.

The Valued Supervisor

A senior pastor who believes in you, and loves you, is one of the most powerful influences in being able to thrive in ministry as an associate staff member.

—A youth pastor

I want to start by thanking you for your concern for your associate staff members. The fact that you are taking time to read this article shows that you care about them and their ministries. May God guide and bless you as you seek to be the kind of ministry supervisor who draws the best from your associate staff members and helps them find deep satisfaction and joy in ministry.

The material in this article is drawn from a two-year study of people who are thriving in associate staff ministry. The study began with a series of focus groups across the United States and Canada with veteran associate staff members in various ministry areas who felt they were thriving in their ministries, not just surviving. A survey based on the findings of these focus groups was developed and sent to veteran associate staff members in 14 U.S. and Canadian denominations. (Details of the study are summarized in appendix C.) The responses provided a clear, strong, consistent picture of what helps associate staff members thrive in ministry. One of the most important influences is how they work with and relate to you, their supervisor.

Helping Your Associate Staff Thrive in Ministry

I don't know if you recognize how influential you are to your associate staff's sense of satisfaction and well-being in ministry. While it is true that each person is to carry out his or her ministry as unto God, not dependent on the praise of others, your leadership, example, encouragement, feedback, and support have a tremendous impact on your associates. You function as an overshepherd, leading, supervising and supporting those who labor with you. When long-term associate staff members were asked what helped them thrive in ministry, one of the first things mentioned was their relationship with you. Directly or indirectly, much of what influences their sense of satisfaction and well-being in ministry is touched somehow by you, their supervisor. When their work relationship with you is positive, they feel trusted, encouraged, supported, affirmed, and motivated for ministry. They feel that they are members of a team, partners with you in ministry, instead of ministry hirelings. They also feel that their ministry areas are valued and given credibility, increasing congregational support. (For a fuller discussion of the benefits of a good work relationship between associate staff members and their supervisors, see chapter 2.)

Strengthening the work relationship between supervisor and associate staff member is an ongoing process that requires the thought and attention of both people. In chapter 2 I discussed issues that associate staff members need to address to meet the needs of their supervisors and to develop a positive relationship in ministry with you. Here I share what you can do to help your associates thrive in their ministries. I'll begin by looking at a dozen things that thriving associate staff members value from their supervisors and then present a few specific practices that may help you respond to their needs. Finally, the chapter closes with some questions for your reflection and for discussion with your associate staff.

What Associate Staff Value from Their Supervisors

When 120 veteran associate staff participating in focus groups were asked what their supervisors did that helped them thrive in their ministries, they enthusiastically described a variety of actions and attitudes they had experienced and benefited from. In the follow-up survey, about 400 veteran associate staff members described the most beneficial things supervisors could do to help associate staff members thrive in their ministries. Their answers clustered in the same 12 areas as those of the focus-group members. If you want to help your associate staff thrive in ministry, these 12 items are important to consider.

1. Help Develop a Sense of Partnership in Ministry

Time and again, thriving associate staff members described working with their supervisor as a partnership in ministry or as serving together as a team. About 90 percent said that their supervisor treats them as a partner in ministry, not just an assistant, and that this attitude and treatment are very important to their longevity and satisfaction in ministry. This issue is foundational to many others that follow. A basic attitude of acceptance and respect creates a climate for ministry that brings out the best in associate staff members and increases their satisfaction in ministry. Here are some ways this kind of climate is developed.

Using labels and language. The titles that associate staff wear influence how people in the congregation perceive them and their work. The labels you use for your associate staff members communicate your valuing of them and their ministries and encourage the respect and support of the congregation. In addition, the language used by supervisors to talk about those they supervise communicates levels of status and value. More than the titles associate staff receive with the job, how you address them and how you talk about them to others can create a team spirit and partnership in ministry together. Talking about "my staff" or "my assistants" does not communicate partnership in ministry; talking about "our ministry team" does.

Developing understanding. Taking time to get to know your associates, their ministry gifts and passions, interests, personalities, and life experiences, communicates that you value them and take their needs and ministries seriously. The better you know them, the better you will understand them and their motivations and goals for ministry. Taking time really to understand your associate staff provides a platform for working well together and helps you work through those times of disappointment or conflict that can easily pull the partnership apart.

Respecting ideas. "Respect" is more than the title of an Aretha Franklin song. It is a basic attitude toward a person that we communicate in many ways. One of the strongest ways to communicate respect to your associates is through how you listen to them and respond to their opinions and ideas as you discuss ministry needs and opportunities together. Listening communicates worth, even if you end up not using the ideas offered. When associate staff members feel that what they have to say is taken seriously, their sense of being part of a ministry team is built up.

Rejoicing together in success. One of the repeated themes that thriving associate staff members discussed was their supervisors' humble attitude and lack of a defensive ego. Their supervisors did not become jealous or envious of their success in ministry, but rejoiced with them when they did well or received praise from people in the congregation. Also, when supervisors received praise from the congregation for ministry successes, they made sure the congregation knew that the associate staff contributed to that success.

Responding with mutual concern and aid. Partnerships in ministry are best demonstrated in how we respond when one member of the team is hurt or struggling. In describing how the Body of Christ is to function, Paul in 1 Corinthians 12:26 states, "And if one member suffers, all the members suffer with it; if one member is honored, all the members rejoice with it." Demonstrating concern for each other and each other's ministries and taking action to assist each other in times of need builds unity on a church staff and creates a sense of partnership in ministry.

2. Lead the Ministry Team Through Vision

While associate staff members want to be viewed and treated as colleagues in ministry, they do value and respect the leadership role of their supervisors. Supervisors have the responsibility of providing leadership to the church and to their associate staff in identifying what they should be doing and how they should go about it. Associate staff members appreciate the supervisor who includes them in this process so they, too, can share the vision for ministry. This inclusion helps them identify how their own areas of ministry relate to the larger picture. This kind of shared planning and commitment make developing ministry strategies, identifying staffing needs, and planning finances easier to accomplish. It is not always easy to do as you are swept along by your daily ministry demands, but regardless of the format, time needs to be *intentionally* set aside to accomplish this task. With this time investment, the staff develops a sense of being a team in ministry together, not just a collection of disjointed ministry specialists.

3. Build Trust Together

Trust is developed over time and is frequently tested. When associate staff members were asked what their supervisors do that is important to their satisfaction and longevity in ministry, two items topped the list: demonstration of trust and belief in their ministry abilities. Many study participants described trust as a two-way street that is strengthened over time as people handle their responsibilities and relationships well. A commitment by both parties is needed to build that trust together and to address promptly any problems that undermine it. Associate staff members describe this kind of trust from supervisors in three ways:

No micromanaging. Associates want to be able to do their work without their supervisor "looking over my shoulder" all the time. The issue is trust in an associate's ability to be a self-starter, to work within the ministry guidelines that stem from the vision and purpose of the church, and to complete the work in a satisfactory manner. When associate staff members are fairly new, they may appreciate extra guidance and feedback, but once they have shown that they can handle their responsibilities, they need to feel trusted with them. Requiring regular progress reports is appropriate, as are encouragement and assistance when difficulties arise. Associate staff want to know that they can turn to the rest of the ministry team if they need help, but that the responsibility still rests on their shoulders.

Receiving appropriate authority. Few things are more frustrating to associate staff than lacking the authority to do the jobs for which they are responsible. They greatly appreciate the supervisor who helps to identify what authority they need to do their work, and who then goes a step further to ensure that they have the ability to exercise it. To deny the associate the appropriate authority needed to do his or her work ensures frustration and failure. Delegation of authority can be developmental, with a little authority being given to an inexperienced staff member, and more given as experience is gained. The authority level should keep pace with the level of responsibility.

Allowing the freedom to fail and learn. Associates need to be able to try new ministry approaches and experience failure as a time to learn, instead of feeling that their judgment and ability are always questioned. How a supervisor responds to occasional failure communicates the level of confidence he or she has in the associate staff member.

4. Be Available and Approachable

Associate staff really value being able to talk with their supervisors about ministry issues. Although they know you are busy with your own ministry demands, and they don't want to intrude when you need to focus on something else, your general availability is important. About 90 percent of the thriving associate staff who participated in this study said that their supervisor's "open-door" policy with them enhanced their ministry satisfaction. They want to be able to discuss ministry problems and to troubleshoot with you. They respect your wisdom and experience, and your knowledge of the congregation; they value your perspective on their work.

I know that supervising pastors are busy and need to establish boundaries to protect their own ability to fulfill their ministry responsibilities. My own senior pastor had an open-door policy with his associate staff, but he also had two ways to protect his time. First, his "open-door" policy was literal—when his door was open, any of the staff could come in to talk. When the door was closed, it was because he needed time to work on something, and we should wait to talk with him later. Second, the church secretary's office was right outside his, and he told her when he needed to be left undisturbed. She helped protect him from impromptu visitors, including those of us on staff.

One more thing needs to be said: Being available is not the same thing as being approachable. Associate staff need to feel that if and when they need to discuss something with you, you will listen to them and respect what they have to say. Proclaiming that your door is always open is not enough. If your associates see you as defensive, argumentative, judgmental, or uncaring, they will hesitate to come to you for advice or help. If you're not sure how you come across to others, get some feedback from someone you respect so that you can see if you are creating the kind of work climate that encourages open communication with associate staff.

5. Support and Encouragement in Ministry

Support and encouragement need to be shown for associate staff members as well as their ministry areas. Some associates minister in ways that are readily seen and affirmed by the congregation. Others work behind the scenes and do not receive the same level of recognition and affirmation.

The supervisor's public recognition and support for each team member, as well as that person's ministries, communicate the value of the ministry and the team member, and greatly encourage those whose low-profile ministries do not receive as much spontaneous appreciation from the congregation.

Some churches have established support teams for staff members, to listen to and respond to their personal needs, help troubleshoot problems they face, and encourage them in their ministries. Other things to consider in supporting your associate staff members include giving them opportunities to be seen by the congregation in the worship service, providing them with public forums to promote their ministries, passing on other people's praise to them, and finding ways to educate the congregation about their work.

6. Care for the Person as Well as the Ministry

Thriving associate staff members report that they feel genuinely loved and cared for by their supervisors. It is not just a matter of caring about their ministries, but also of caring for them as persons. Showing interest in their personal and family life, encouraging them to take time away for spiritual renewal and strengthening family bonds, taking time in meetings for sharing and praying about personal needs—all communicate concern for them as individuals.

One practical way to care for your associates is to allow a flexible work schedule so that they can adjust their time in the office according to the demands of evening meetings, weekend events, and family needs. Being able to take a morning off after a number of evenings out at meetings and having the freedom to attend a son's or daughter's school event in the afternoon demonstrate the church's care for them as persons.

Another way to care for your associates is to be an advocate for them to the church governing boards regarding salaries and benefits. One major source of stress for associate staff members is the effort to provide adequately for themselves and their families. As their supervisor, you have the opportunity and responsibility to bring their needs to the church and to see that they are adequately provided for. Although there are many ways of calculating compensation levels for associate staff members, one good benchmark is the salary and benefits that public-school teachers in your community with comparable education and experience receive. Keep in mind that schoolteachers work only about a nine-month year compared to your associate staff member's 12-month responsibility. Be sure to address health benefits and retirement pay, as well as basic salary.

7. Demonstrate Loyalty

Associate staff members feel a great vote of confidence in their ministries when they know that their supervisors believe in them and will stand by them when others criticize. They need to know that someone is there to back them up when criticism comes. They are looking not for blind loyalty but for an expression of confidence in them that is not easily shaken. They want to know that when criticism is voiced, you will investigate it and listen to their perspective, rather than automatically siding with the person bringing the complaint. Some associates value having their supervisors as a buffer, receiving the criticism and sorting it out with them. Others value having their supervisors refer all critics directly to them, not listening to the complaint until it has been brought directly to the associate staff member. Discuss this matter with your associates to determine how you want to handle such criticism. The major issue is the confidence expressed when you support your associate staff members in the face of criticism, deferring judgment until you have a chance to talk the issue over with them.

8. Keep Communication Open

Open communication is important to any team's ability to work well together. For those who serve in multiple-staff churches, open communication is critical to maintaining cooperative and unified ministry. Many excellent materials are available on improving communication, and the range of issues involved is enormous. I will focus on raising a handful of other issues for your reflection and further consideration.

First, associate staff members are greatly encouraged when you take the time and effort to listen to them and demonstrate that you value their opinions and insights, even if you disagree. I know what it is like to be asked for my ideas for addressing a ministry need, only to have those ideas immediately shot down and my motives attacked. That experience made me much more cautious and guarded in talking with that supervisor. I also know how motivating it is to have my supervisor actively draw out my thoughts and weigh them carefully. That encourages my best efforts to think and share my ideas.

Second, associate staff look to their supervisors to clarify ministry expectations and to help them respond to the variety of ministry opportunities and demands. Ongoing discussion is needed to clarify your expectations. Also, associate staff members need your guidance on what they can do to work well together with you and others on staff. What do you expect of them as you work together? What would help make your job as supervisor easier?

Third, associates appreciate supervisors who keep them informed of developments that have the potential to affect their ministry areas. Having the information necessary to make wise decisions and not being surprised by some announcement at a board or congregational meeting are important to their ministry satisfaction.

Fourth, associates appreciate supervisors who season their communication with a sense of humor. With so much stress in ministry, finding humor in the midst of ministry demands lightens the heart and helps keep discouragement at bay.

Fifth, associate staff members long for the ability to speak openly and honestly with their supervisors, sharing the ups and downs of ministry instead of constantly striving to be perceived as being on top of everything and in control. The ability to be open and authentic takes time to develop, but little will happen without your example. Mutual support and prayer can happen at a deeper level, strengthening your commitment to each other's ministry success.

Finally, as disagreements or disappointments occur between staff members, associate staff value supervisors who do not allow these things to fester, disrupting the ability to communicate and work well together. As difficult as it may be, associates appreciate supervisors who address the conflicts or hurts and lead in the process of reconciliation. This action may take great measures of patience and grace, but you will have the associate's greater respect when the issues are resolved. When conflicts on staff are properly addressed, they can become an occasion for drawing you closer together.

9. Give Constructive Feedback

Associate staff members appreciate constructive feedback on their ministry efforts. Although none of us likes to hear criticism, it is easier to receive
it and respond positively when we trust the motives of our evaluator. Constructive feedback is critical to the ongoing growth and development of
your associate staff. Too many churches do not have a good process in
place to help the staff grow in effectiveness through evaluation. One of the
most loving tasks you can undertake for your associates is to develop and
implement such a process. Here are a few guidelines:

First, feedback should be given on a regular basis, not just at an annual
performance review. Part of your role as supervisor is to provide ongoing
feedback to your associates on what you believe is going well, their strengths
in ministry, and areas for growth and improvement.

Second, start with the associate's self-evaluation and then provide your
perspective. More often than not, associate staff members are aware of
the problem areas in their ministries. If they bring it up, it will be easier for
you to discuss it together and seek ways to help them through it.

Third, focus first and foremost on associates' strengths, gifts, and ministry accomplishments; then gently tackle one or two growth areas at a
time. It's important that your associates maintain hope in the process and
perceive your positive regard for their ability. Focusing too much on what
needs to improve can be discouraging, undermining the motivation and energy necessary to move forward.

Fourth, make sure that your feedback focuses on their ministry efforts
and strategies, not just on end results. Circumstances outside their control
may have influenced the final outcomes. Help them see the good in their
efforts even if the outcome was less than what either of you had hoped for.
Finally, if major problems need to be addressed, patiently walk with them
through the process, even if it results in their eventual resignation from the
church staff. I will never forget working with one senior pastor as we met
for weeks with a staff member I supervised, discussing our growing differences in ministry philosophy and the perceived problems in his ministry
area. The senior pastor patiently listened to, encouraged, prayed with, and
confronted the staff member over a few months. When the decision was
reached that he should leave, it was a mutual one, and he was able to do so
with the support of the church.

10. Be a Model and Mentor in Ministry

Associate staff members want to work with someone they can respect. It is far easier to receive direction and constructive feedback from a respected superior. Three key aspects stand out in a supervisor associate staff can respect.

First, they are looking for a spiritual leader to be an example to them. You don't need to try to appear perfect, because they value your honest sharing of spiritual struggles. They are looking for someone who has a heart that seeks God and a commitment to carry out ministry in ways that honor God. They want a brother or sister in the Lord whom they can learn from, be encouraged by, and follow in ministry.

Second, they are looking for a person of integrity to follow, someone who is the same in public settings as in private meetings. They want to work under a person who strives to live by what she believes, who does not compromise personal commitments, and who is quick to repent and confess wrong attitudes or actions.

Third, they are looking for a person who is willing to learn and grow in ministry. This kind of positive model encourages their own motivation to grow and to be mentored by you and others. These three aspects encourage your associate staff to give their best efforts to their ministries and to follow your leadership.

11. Encourage Personal and Professional Development

Thriving associate staff members in this study described how their supervisors encourage them to keep learning and growing personally and professionally. This support and encouragement prevent them from stagnating and renew their energies for ministry. Encouragement for growth includes a number of areas—retreats for spiritual growth and vitality; professional conferences for networking, encouragement and skill development; continuing formal study at the graduate level; marriage-enrichment seminars; and other ministry workshops and continuing-education opportunities.

Two ways that you can encourage this ongoing development are to fan the motivation to grow and serve God more effectively and to provide the opportunities to do so. Igniting your associates' desire to grow in ministry comes through your own example and your affirmation and active encouragement of their participation in growth activities. Providing the opportunities requires that the church make time available, provide financial support, and help find information about what is available. Work with your church board to develop policies that encourage the ongoing development of the staff through setting aside time and money for conferences and other continuing-education opportunities. Encourage your associates to identify the professional associations in their ministry areas and other formal and informal educational opportunities from which they can benefit. Don't forget to look for personal-enrichment opportunities that can renew them and facilitate growth. Make sure these are acceptable for church support as well. A listing of associate staff professional organizations is available in appendix D.

12. Pray for and with Them

I began this section by focusing on the foundational issue of developing a sense of partnership in ministry. I now close it with another foundational issue, your prayer support for your associate staff. This is not lip service to what I think is "spiritually correct," but a recognition of a vital part of healthy multiple-staff ministry that influences many other areas. I know the difference between serving on a church staff where we prayed together for each other, and where we did not. I have felt the impact of that prayer, or lack of prayer, as I tackled my ministry assignments. I know the power of encouragement and support, and the ways I have seen God work when we as a staff prayed together for the needs of the church, our ministries, and our personal struggles. Prayer draws a staff together in support of each other and in recognition that God must supply the wisdom, direction, and power for ministry effectiveness. Prayer binds us together as we seek to follow God in service to the church and the communities in which we live. Praying together keeps our focus on God's ability to guide and provide.

Whatever else you do from the list of items above, commit yourself to pray for and with your associate staff. *Pray for them*, and tell them you are praying for them. Find out what they would like you to pray for and do so. Ask them to share how God answers those prayers and rejoice with them. *Pray with them* and let them pray for you. Take time during the week to share together and pray together for each other, your ministries, and the needs of the church. *Pray in public* for your associates. Lift them and their ministries up and encourage others to pray for them as well. *Pray in private* for your associates, asking God to strengthen, guide, protect and bless them as they serve in the church. Enlist others to pray for them, so that each staff member knows that there are people in the church to whom they can turn for prayer support.

Practices That Strengthen Staff Relationships

Regular Staff Meetings

Because of the importance of open, ongoing communication, the need to develop a united team effort in ministry, and the power of mutual encouragement and prayer, regular staff meetings can be one of the best investments of your time with your associate staff. Carving out time in the schedule to meet weekly and making it a priority for all staff members help foster a sense of being part of a ministry team. Most of you probably already have regular meetings with your associates. Let me recommend five elements of a staff meeting that can be of great benefit to you and your associate staff.

Refocus the vision. The daily demands of ministry can blur your staff's vision of what they are striving for. Take time together to renew your vision of what God has called your church and your staff to be and do. This "vision refresher" can increase motivation for ministry. It will also help in the rest of your meeting as you review ministry efforts and needs and determine what should be done next.

Debrief ministry efforts, needs, goals. With each staff member working in different ministry areas, time should be taken to allow each person to report on what's been happening, what successes and difficulties are being faced, and what needs and goals they are addressing. This means that the agenda for your staff meetings comes from all the staff, not just you. As each person contributes to the staff meeting, ownership of the meeting and interest in each other's ministries grow.

Troubleshoot together. As difficulties are raised by various staff members, determine which issues should be tackled by the group together and which should be dealt with in some other setting. One benefit of troubleshooting ministry problems together is the development of mutual concern and care for each other and for each other's ministries. Later, as good things happen in those ministry areas, the whole staff rejoices. There is also much wisdom in your staff that each member can benefit from. Encouraging them to assist each other builds their unity and commitment to each other.

Pray together. Whatever else you do, don't neglect this important aspect of meeting together. Staff members need to know that they are supported in prayer, both in their ministry responsibilities and in their personal needs. Staff meetings that focus all on reporting, planning, and troubleshooting, but neglect prayer, can be a draining and discouraging experience. Take time to pray together for your staff's needs and those of the church. If your staff is large, consider varying how you do this, praying together sometimes and praying in pairs at other times. Over time, this practice will allow you to pray individually with each staff member. Believe me, that can mean a lot to your associates and to your growing unity as a ministry team. Finally, as you see prayers answered, take time to revisit them and give thanks and praise to God together. Reviewing how God has worked and worshipping together strengthen faith and hope to face future difficult times.

Learn together. A staff benefits from studying and learning together. Taking time for this activity may seem an impossibility with everything else that needs to be done, but the benefits can be tremendous. Take time to study Scripture together, and relate it to personal or ministry concerns. Building a strong biblical foundation for life and ministry can influence a lifetime of ministry. Taking time to read and study relevant books dealing with societal needs or ministry approaches can challenge your ministry team to consider how better to minister in your community. Studying together allows you to build common ground in your convictions, ministry philosophies, and goals. This strengthens your unity in ministry and focuses your efforts toward common ends. It is a worthwhile investment of your time.

Staff and Personal Retreats

All ministry positions have their share of stresses and problems. As you and your associates carry out your ministries, it is easy to become worn out, drained by the constant demands of the job. Your spiritual vitality can suffer periods of dryness, or a sense of becoming routine. Having times to "retreat" for renewal and growth can help a staff member thrive in ministry over the long haul. Carving out time for this can seem nearly impossible, but it needs to become a priority to help everyone remain spiritually healthy and effective in ministry. Stephen Covey[1] likens taking time for personal renewal to sharpening a saw. You can cut more wood, with less work, with a sharp saw than you can with a dull one. The time invested sharpening the saw is worth the effort. Consider ways you can help your associate staff with their personal spiritual renewal through retreat opportunities.

Staff retreats. Taking time away together as a staff can help build friendships and mutual support for each other. Some retreats can focus on vision and goals for ministry and on building unity together. Others can focus more on personal spiritual health and growth, allowing you to support each other in keeping your relationship with God vital and taking steps toward greater spiritual maturity. Whatever focus your retreat has, make sure there is time together for fun and relationship-building. Don't turn it into one long staff meeting. If time and money for a staff retreat are not already available to you, you may need to discuss this plan with your church board, helping board members to see the potential benefits for your staff's effectiveness in ministry.

Personal retreats. Providing opportunities for your associates to take time away for personal retreats can boost their spiritual vitality. While extended time away (a few days) can be helpful, even a day or less away to read Scripture, pray, and be in fellowship with God can be renewing to the spirit. Consider developing a policy that allows staff members to take time for personal retreats, and check within your congregation and denomination to identify free or inexpensive places where staff members could go for a day or an overnight. Lead by example in this area, and tell how it benefits you. Your example can encourage your associates to take time for a retreat as well.

Time Off-Task: Socializing Together

Associate staff members value the opportunity to get to know their supervisor, and a supervisor's effort to get to know them. When church staffs take time to know each other, they build bridges that encourage open communication, mutual understanding, and a sense of acceptance. Having occasional meals together, taking time in staff meetings for personal sharing and prayer, throwing birthday parties, sharing recreational activities together—all provide opportunities to get to know each other better and foster a supportive fellowship in ministry. You don't have to be best friends and you don't have to share the same hobbies to build positive relationships that help you work well together.

One of my senior pastors was a marvelous example in this regard. We took time in our staff meetings for personal sharing as well as church ministry issues. He hosted Christmas dinners and summer cookouts for the staff and their spouses. These casual times and special events helped us all know each other better. We became friends and respected each other in ministry, despite our many differences. These activities went a long way to help us work through conflicts that arose in our ministry together.

Celebrations

I have to confess, this last recommendation does not come directly from this study of thriving associate staff members, but from my own observations and convictions about encouraging people in ministry. Two aspects of congregational ministry can undermine a person's motivation and sense of accomplishment. First, much of what we are seeking to accomplish is hard to measure and develops over long periods of time. Progress is hard to identify at times, and maintaining energy for ministry when we cannot see clear results can be difficult. Second, the daily demands of ministry can keep us so busy that we do not take time to reflect on the good things that have been accomplished. We're so busy "doing the ministry" that we do not take time to rejoice over what God has done in and through the church. These two things can dull one's ability to find joy in ministry. Allow me to propose a simple remedy.

I have become a great believer in the power of celebrations. Just as the nation of Israel used festivals to remember what God had done and to give praise for divine love and mercy, we who serve on church staffs need times to recognize what God has done and to give praise for it. What the church and church staff need is more celebrations! We will find much to be thankful for if we look around us and see how God is working in our congregations and communities. There is much to celebrate as your associate staff members pour their energies into their ministry areas—people coming to faith in Christ, people moving forward in discipleship, new people coming to the church, big events going well, volunteers recruited and equipped for ministry, financial resources given to support ministry efforts, people worshipping the Lord. It's too easy to keep our focus on our never-ending needs in ministry and neglect to rejoice as God provides for us and works in our midst. As a supervisor, consider how you can celebrate with your associates what God is doing.

Taking Inventory: Questions for Reflection and Discussion

Some of the questions that follow may be good for you to reflect on privately, others may be good to discuss with your associates. Your ministry situation is unique, and these questions may trigger other issues that would be more helpful for you to consider. Use these questions in ways that will be of the most assistance to you and to your associates. (Additional questions for discussion with your associates can be found at the end of chapter 2.)

Partnership in Ministry

1. How do you view those you supervise in ministry? If it is hard to feel that they are really partners in ministry, what do you think is preventing that sense of partnership from developing?

2. Do their titles encourage congregational support and respect for them and their ministries?

3. Does the language you use convey to them and to others a sense of being part of a ministry team?

4. How well have you gotten to know your staff as people? What kinds of things could you do together to get to know each other better?

5. In what ways is your respect for your associate staff expressed? Are there things you do that might communicate a lack of respect for staff or their ideas?

6. How do you find yourself reacting when people praise your associate staff? Is your reaction something you need to seek God's help to correct?

Leading Through Vision

1. Have you clearly articulated your understanding of God's purpose and vision for your church? Have you shared it with your associates and taken time to help them identify how their ministries tie into and support the larger vision?

2. Are you setting time aside on some kind of regular schedule to revisit your vision for ministry and use it to help focus your ministry efforts?

Building Trust

1. How are you feeling right now about the trustworthiness of your associate staff? What issues would need to be addressed before your trust in them could be strong?

2. As you think over the last few months or years, is there anything that you have done that might be hindering your associates' ability to trust you as their supervisor? What steps could you take to restore that trust?

3. Do you find yourself checking up on your associates' work a lot? Why do you think you do this? If your associate staff need to gain ministry experience and skill, how can you help them work toward more independence in their work?

4. How do you react when your associates fail in some aspect of their ministries? How could you help them deal with their own sense of failure and learn from these experiences?

Availability and Approachability

1. How available are you to your associate staff? In what ways can you communicate your desire to be available to them when needed, but also protect the time you need to fulfill your own ministry responsibilities?

2. Do you have a sense of how approachable you are as a person? How do you deal with criticism or complaints from others?

3. Is there anything you can do to communicate better your desire to have your associates share freely with you their ideas, concerns, and frustrations?

Support and Encouragement

1. Do you have a sense of how much encouragement your associate staff members receive from others in the church? If you suspect that they may need more, how might you go about providing it?

2. Are there regular opportunities for your congregation to see and hear from your associate staff regarding their areas of ministry?

3. Do you publicly talk about your associate staff and their ministries, encouraging others to pray for them and support their efforts?

4. Would your associate staff members appreciate having a lay-support team meet with them to encourage them and address their needs in ministry?

Caring for the Person

1. Do you find yourself occupied primarily with how well your associates' ministries are going and not paying much attention to how they are doing personally?

2. Are there regular times when you and your associates share and pray together for both ministry and personal needs?

3. In what ways are you communicating to your associates how important they are to you and your concern for their well-being?

4. Is there flexibility in your associates' schedules to allow them to have time with their families, especially when evening and weekend ministry demands are heavy?

5.   Are you an advocate to the church governing board to provide a fair salary and benefit package for your associate staff?

Demonstrating Loyalty

1.   How have you responded when someone has come to you with criticism of your associates? Did your response demonstrate loyalty to your associates and concern for them?

2.   Would your associates prefer to have people come directly to them with criticisms, or come to you first as their supervisor?

Open Communication

1.   Does how you listen demonstrate that you are genuinely interested in your associates' ideas, opinions, and insights?

2.   Are you clear in communicating your expectations of your associate staff members?

3.   Do you keep your associates informed of matters that have the potential to affect their ministry areas?

4.   Do you find yourself being intense and serious all the time with your associates, or do you find ways to allow humor to lighten the work atmosphere?

5.   What level of transparency characterizes how you and your associates talk with each other? Would your ability to work well together be enhanced by greater authenticity than what you have now? How might you begin moving in that direction?

6.   How do you tend to deal with conflicts and hurts with your associates? Are there any unresolved hurts that need to be addressed for reconciliation? What do you fear might happen if you try to resolve this now?

Constructive Feedback

1. Do you have a process in place to help your associates evaluate their own ministries and receive constructive feedback from you?

2. Is evaluation a regular part of your work together with your associates?

3. When you have conducted evaluations, have you focused primarily on associates' strengths and successes in ministry, helping them identify and work on one or two growth areas at a time?

Model and Mentor

1. Are you comfortable with the idea that your associate staff members look to you to be an example to them in spiritual growth, ministry integrity, and openness to learn? Is there anything that you fear will cause them to lose respect for you as their leader? What steps can you take to address this concern?

Personal and Professional Development

1. Do you encourage your associates to take regular advantage of continuing-education opportunities, to participate in professional organizations, and to benefit from personal growth opportunities?

2. Does your church provide staff with time and money to do the kinds of things listed in the previous question? If not, what steps could you take to encourage the church to do more in this area?

Prayer

1. Do you regularly pray for and with your associate staff members? Do you pray for both their ministry and their personal needs? Do you let them know that you are praying for them?

2. Do you encourage others in your church to pray for your associate staff members as well?

Staff Meetings and Retreats

1. Do we meet weekly as a staff to refocus our vision for ministry; debrief our ministry efforts, needs, and goals; troubleshoot ministry problems together; pray together; and learn together? Which of these areas are our strengths, and which ones should we take more time to do together?

2. Have we ever had a retreat together as a staff? If so, how did it benefit us? If not, how might this kind of experience benefit us as a ministry team? Where could we go that would not be too expensive? How can we carve out time for a retreat?

3. Can we provide opportunities for the church staff to take personal retreats once or more a year? Again, how can we get the church to provide the time and money? What resources do we have nearby to take advantage of?

Socializing and Celebrating

1. Do we as a staff take time for socializing, enjoying time together away from the church office? What kinds of mutual interests do we have that we might pursue together?

2. What kinds of events (e.g., holidays, birthdays, sporting events) might we use as excuses to get together and have a good time together with our families?

3. Do we take time as a staff to reflect on what God has done in our church and to celebrate it together? How could we make this a regular part of our staff meetings?

Feedback to and from Your Associates

Here are a number of questions that you may want to ask your associate staff members. You may learn a lot just by taking the time to listen to their responses and encouraging them to ask questions for your response.

1. What three to five things could I do as your supervisor that would help you as you carry out your ministry responsibilities?

2. What three to five things could your associates do that would help you most as their supervisor?

3. When we have disagreements about ministry issues, how do we want to deal with them to best work through them?

4. What kinds of things could we do that would help in building a cooperative ministry together?

5. Are there any areas where one or the other of us has felt that trust or loyalty in our work relationship has been compromised? Has anything taken place that has caused our respect for each other to suffer? If so, what can we do to resolve them?

---

1. Stephen R. Covey, *The 7 Habits of Highly Effective People* (New York: Simon & Schuster, 1989), 287.

The Supportive Church Board

A few of the kids in our youth group were going through some really tough times, and one of the elders came to me and said, "Let me know if there is anything I can do to help. I've got your back covered." That kind of support from the church means a lot!

—A youth pastor

After serving as an associate staff member in churches for 11 years, I moved into teaching Christian education at a seminary in Canada. While my family and I were there, I had to adjust to no longer being a church staff member. That was a growing experience for me, as I gained a new perspective on being a part of the Body of Christ, and an appreciation of the pressures of being an active layman in the church. After two years of volunteer service in the church's educational ministries, I became an elder, serving on the governing board of the church. It was quite a challenge, as we sought to work with and support our pastoral staff and together guide the church in its ministries. One concern that I developed during that time was how we as the church governing board could support and encourage our associate staff members. We were so used to working with the senior pastor that we did not often spend much time considering the needs of other staff members. Unfortunately, this pattern seems to be all too typical.

In most churches, the supervision and support of associate staff rest entirely in the hands of the senior pastor. While your senior pastor or other associate staff supervisor has the most direct responsibility for supervising and supporting the associate staff, there are still things that lay leaders can do to enhance their ministry experience and effectiveness.

This appendix is written for those who serve as lay leaders in their church governing structure. In some churches, this may be an elder board, while others have sessions, administrative boards, church councils, or deacon boards. Whatever your church's structure, if you have responsibility to oversee ministry and personnel, this material is for you. Throughout, I will use the term "board" to describe your group.

I want to suggest ways that you and your board can support your church's associate staff members, helping them to serve with deep satisfaction. By supporting them, encouraging them, stretching them, and caring for them, you can invest in their ministry and help them thrive where God has placed them.

These insights emerged from a two-year study of long-term associate staff members who are thriving in their ministries. Through focus-group discussions and a survey of veteran associate staff members in 14 denominations in the United States and Canada, we have gained an inside look at what contributes to their satisfaction, personal well-being, and longevity in ministry. (Details of the study are summarized in appendix C.) Over 400 survey respondents described what their supervisors and church boards can do to help them thrive in ministry. Their responses have been grouped and summarized below, with questions for your reflection and discussion provided at the conclusion.

Thank you for caring enough about your church staff to read and act on these suggestions. May God guide you as you carry out your important role of leadership in your church and as you support and care for those who serve with you.

1. Create A Supportive Ministry Environment

It is important to understand how great an impact the working environment can have on workers' motivation, effort, and satisfaction with their work. When people feel supported, respected, and provided with the resources needed to get their work done, they feel energized and motivated to do it well, even in the face of challenges and problems. When the work setting is characterized by a lack of unity, support, and respect, motivation is hard to maintain and discouragement can easily set in. Your church's associate staff members will face many challenges in their ministries; at times they will feel discouraged and wonder if they are doing the right thing by serving here. The ministry environment that you and their direct ministry supervisor help create can make a big difference in their ability to persevere through the challenges, see God's work, and find deep satisfaction in their own work. Here are some specific things that you and your church board can do to help.

Focus on Keeping the Church Healthy

An excellent place to start is to realize that the general "relational health" of your church has a great impact on all of your staff members as they carry out their ministries. A church where there is unity in ministry vision, where church members understand the importance of finding ways to use their gifts in the Body, where political maneuvering is discouraged, and where people are able to work through hurts and disagreements and keep bitterness from gaining a foothold—that is the kind of environment that allows your staff members to focus their attention and energies on their ministry responsibilities. By paying attention to maintaining the health of the congregation, your board is providing a supportive environment for your pastor and associate staff. Make sure that with all the major initiatives, decisions, and projects your board addresses, you do not lose sight of the need to promote the health of your congregation as members relate and work together in ministry. Everything you do in this area benefits both your church and your staff.

Affirm and Encourage Your Staff

When veteran associate staff members described what helped them thrive in ministry, near the top of the list was that the church's lay leadership supported and believed in them and affirmed their gifts for ministry. They also benefited greatly from receiving words or notes of appreciation and encouragement from those to whom they ministered. With the frequent stresses of their ministries, and the fact that much of what they do may be carried out "behind the scenes," your verbal affirmation, appreciation, and encouragement can be a powerful boost to how they feel about themselves and their ministries. Paul tells us to "encourage one another and build up one another, just as you also are doing" (1 Thess. 5:11). Your board can have a ministry of encouragement to your associate staff. When you tell them that you believe in them, respect them, support them, recognize their gifts, and appreciate their ministries, you encourage their hearts. While God's affirmation of them is of utmost importance, God can use you to help them see how important they are to your church.

Build Support in the Congregation

When associate staff members feel that their congregations value and support them and their ministry efforts, it boosts their motivation to do their best. Strong congregational support for associate staff can be built in many ways. Look over the suggestions that follow, and see which ones are possible in your congregation.

First, the title and ordination or licensing status that associate staff members carry can influence how congregation members will view and respond to them. In our culture, titles communicate something about the status of people and their work. Titles such as "pastor" or "minister" imply greater status than "director" or "leader." In addition, staff members who are ordained or licensed by their church or denomination may be viewed with a level of respect that is not given to non-ordained or licensed staff. The attempt here is not to strive for higher status or to wield greater power, but to encourage congregation members to respect, value, and support those who serve on the church staff. Using titles that encourage respect can help your staff. Providing opportunities for recognition of ministry calling, preparation, and gifts through ordination or licensing can also promote congregational support for your associates. Some denominations have guidelines on titles or ordination tied to educational preparation, type of ministry responsibilities, gender, and confirmation of gifts and calling. Take a look at what your church is able to do and find ways to promote respect for your associates and their ministries in the congregation. Even if ordination or licensing is not possible, a congregational commissioning service can help build support for your associate staff members in their ministries.

Second, provide opportunities for your associate staff to be seen and heard by the congregation. For some associate staff, such as a minister of music, this happens naturally every week. For others, such as a youth pastor or children's pastor, it may take intentional planning. Public recognition and support for your associates grow with public exposure. For churches with large associate staffs, this may mean developing a schedule for them to take turns helping with some aspect of public worship. However you do it, find ways for your congregation to see and hear from your associate staff on a regular basis.

Third, find ways to educate the congregation about what your associate staff members do and its importance. While you may have a good understanding of what staff members do in their ministries, many in your congregation may not. It is often a mystery, especially if the associate's work is "behind the scenes" rather than up-front on Sunday morning. When your congregation understands and values the work your associate staff does, a sense of support grows that your associates can feel. Highlighting their ministries in the church newsletter is one way to keep the congregation informed and to build support for associate staff.

Fourth, highlight the associate staff's ministry efforts and achievements and encourage congregation members to share words or notes of appreciation with them. Receiving this affirmation from those whom they labor to serve on God's behalf means a lot to associate staff. Taking time in public gatherings to recognize and affirm the ministries of your associate staff is a good way to "prime the pump" of encouragement.

Provide Needed Ministry Resources

A congregation that provides associate staff members with the authority and resources needed to carry out their ministries demonstrates a high level of respect for them as ministers and the importance of their work. Conversely, when a staff member is given a ministry responsibility but lacks the resources to do it well, mixed signals are sent about the importance of that ministry to the church. Your church board has the responsibility of making sure that the church staff has what is needed to fulfill ministry responsibilities. Take a look at your budget and what it communicates to your associate staff members. Do they have what they need to do the job?

Connect and Have Fellowship

Take time to get to know your church's associate staff members. It's easy for church board members to focus on getting to know the senior pastor, but the associate staff can benefit from your personal interest and encouragement as well. Take time to know them as people, not just staff members. Help them and their families to feel loved and appreciated for who they are, not just for what they do for the church. Help them feel a part of the church body, not just employees. This effort will go a long way toward building a team spirit and making their ministry with you a source of satisfaction.

Provide Prayer Support

For those on your staff, knowing that you, as the lay leaders of the church, are supporting their ministry efforts and personal needs in prayer is a great encouragement. Take time in your meetings to pray for and with them. Make this a regular part of your agenda. As individual board members, pray for them during the week on a regular basis. Take time to talk with them outside your meetings and ask how you can support them in prayer. Occasionally take time with them individually to pray for them and their ministries. Prayer builds a sense of partnership in ministry and encourages the heart. It is a means by which God allows us to join in the task of meeting the needs of others. Make this a top priority for how you will support your associate staff.

2. Allow Associate Staff the Opportunity to Lead

Providing a supportive environment is an important beginning, but how you actually work with and respond to your church's associate staff members as they carry out their ministries can contribute to their satisfaction or discouragement. Here are three ways that you can encourage your associate staff to exercise proper leadership in their ministries and find satisfaction in the process.

Clarify Job Description and Expectations

The senior pastor or other staff supervisor may take the lead, but it is important that you as a board and the associate staff members are on the same page regarding their ministry responsibilities and the church's expectations of them as staff members. A common understanding reduces conflicts and misunderstandings, helping staff members know where and when they can exercise authority and when they need to seek approval from their ministry supervisor or the board to act. Misunderstandings in these areas create headaches, frustration, and discouragement. Preventing miscommunication is a worthwhile investment of time and effort. Take time at your board meetings to review each staff member's responsibilities and how you expect them to be carried out. Also, review your responsibilities toward staff and what staff members should be able to expect from you.

Be Open to New Ideas and Risks

Associate staff members appreciate ministry supervisors and church boards that trust them enough to let them explore and try out new ministry approaches. They want to be able to explore ways to make their ministries more effective, not just maintain the status quo. This exploration requires that the church leadership grant them some ability to take initiative and the freedom to take risks. As associate staff members mature in their ministries, they need to feel that they are trusted to exercise more authority in initiating changes in how their ministries are carried out. Some ideas will meet with success, others will not. For associate staff members to thrive in their ministries, they have to be able to take some risks without feeling that their job is on the line every time something doesn't go right. A degree of freedom to fail encourages initiative and creativity, opening the way toward increased ministry effectiveness.

Allow Input into the Broader Ministry of the Church

As time goes on and associate staff members gain ministry experience and knowledge of the congregation and community, they appreciate church leaders' inviting and listening to their input on ministry issues outside their direct area of responsibility. It is a vote of confidence in them as leaders in the church whose insights and perspectives are respected. Many such opportunities will occur in church staff meetings as the staff discusses ministry needs. However, this interchange can also be encouraged by allowing the associate staff to participate to some degree in the meetings of the church board.

Some churches include their associate staff as members of their board, while others allow them to attend part or all of the meetings but do not allow them to vote. Still others do not include them on the board at all. Of the thriving associate staff members who participated in this study, about 75 percent attend board meetings, and 50 percent of those are voting members. Whatever your policy and practices, let me encourage you to consider at least doing the following:

a) Provide a time at your board meetings when associate staff members can share a report of how their ministries are going, including the needs or challenges they face and the good things that are happening. (If you have many associate staff members, this may have to be done on a rotating basis.)

b) Where appropriate, make them aware of the issues the board is dealing with and ask if they have any questions or insights to share.

c) Take time to pray with them for personal and ministry needs.

Doing these things helps build a good working relationship between associates and board, keeps them informed of issues that may have an impact on their ministry areas, provides them a chance to share their perspectives and be heard, and encourages unity in prayer together.

If you do have associate staff members attend board meetings when ministry policies and plans are being discussed, be sure to create an environment that encourages them to share what they really think about the items you are discussing. You will want to confirm this practice with your senior pastor, and not all will be equally comfortable with the idea, but there is value in having this kind of openness in board discussions. Sometimes associate staff don't say what they think for fear it will be contrary to their senior pastor's views, and they don't want to appear disloyal or divisive. From my perspective, loyalty is not shown by being a "yes-man" (or yes-woman) in the decision-making process, but by how you stand by and support the decisions of the senior pastor and board once they are made. If an associate staff member has concerns about a decision being made by the board and does not make these concerns known, that I would consider disloyal. However, once a decision is made, the associate staff member must support the board in its decision and not complain about it to others.

3. Provide Opportunities for Growth and Renewal

Associate staff members appreciate serving in churches that allow them opportunities to continue to grow in ministry vision and skills. They value being exposed to new ideas and ways of doing ministry, being challenged to evaluate their ministries and finding ways to be more effective, and having time for their own spiritual renewal. As a church board, consider how you can invest in the ongoing growth and renewal of all of your staff members. Here are some things that associate staff members say they benefit from most.

Continuing Education Is a Must

Associate staff members want to keep learning and growing in ministry effectiveness. Having the time and money available to attend professional conferences, take classes at a local seminary or university, participate in ministry workshops, or even to pursue a graduate degree in their ministry area makes possible these growth opportunities. Consider how your board could make continuing-education opportunities available to staff. These experiences help motivate them and renew their energies, as well as providing them with new ideas and insights that can promote increased ministry effectiveness. It's an investment in both your staff members and your church. Make sure you provide them with both the time and money to make these benefits possible.

Support a Growing Vision for Ministry

Every associate staff member comes into a church with a vision of what her ministry can be. As time progresses, her understanding of the needs and resources of the congregation and community grows, and her ministry vision grows and changes as well. Your board can be of great help in this process. You can start by helping staff members understand the church's vision for ministry and how their own ministry area ties into the larger picture. Encourage your associate staff people to share their vision for ministry with you, and as you see them dreaming about a possible future, support them in exploring what steps need to be taken to get there. Your associate staff members don't want to do just "ministry maintenance." They want to be used by God to help the church extend its outreach and improve its ministry effectiveness. Encourage them to keep pursuing this aim, and help them persevere as they work toward it.

Allow for a Dynamic Job Description

Associate staff members find that the demands of their jobs change over time, and new opportunities come for them to exercise their gifts and abilities in ways that were not part of the original job description. They appreciate the opportunity to have a "dynamic" job description that allows them to respond to changing ministry demands and opportunities. It also allows for growth on the job and for God to draw out new gifts for ministry. Some measure of flexibility and opportunities to review and revise the job description over time are appreciated. Don't expect the job descriptions of your associate staff to remain static, but encourage regular times for evaluation and the assessment of new ministry needs. Allow the ministry gifts of your staff to blossom on the job.

Encourage Personal and Staff Retreats

Spiritual growth and renewal are a must for those who serve on staff in your church. Your staff members face many stresses in ministry, and they can easily find themselves caring for the spiritual needs of others and not having adequate time available for their own spiritual nurture. Encourage your staff to take time for both group and individual retreats for spiritual renewal. Help associates to locate retreat sites and provide funding to make it possible. This is a critical investment that pays off in the ministries that flow out of their walk with God.

Also, consider an annual joint retreat of board and staff. The focus of this retreat should not be business or ministry issues, but growth together in your walk with God. These kinds of experiences can unite you in your ministry vision and build bonds of fellowship that enhance your ability to minister together.

4. Respond to Associates' Personal Needs

Your associate staff members are employees of the church, but they are also your brothers and sisters in Christ, and members of your fellowship. It is important to see them as people God has called you to care for, not just supervise. There are several ways that your board can respond to the personal and family needs of your associate staff members, helping them thrive as they serve your congregation.

Provide Adequate Compensation and Benefits

Associate staff members who feel that they are thriving in their work report that their churches pay them adequate salary and benefits to provide for themselves and their families. Unfortunately, one reason that some associate staff members look for new ministry positions or leave church staff ministry altogether is a lack of adequate pay. Associate staff have a basic need to afford to live in your community and to meet the needs of their families. As their families grow and financial demands increase, they sometimes find that their church salaries do not keep pace. How is your church doing in this area?

Churches often stretch their budgets to bring on new associate staff members, and they may be unsure what kind of compensation package is fair. They may also find themselves fighting the temptation to pay as little as they can to get or keep someone. If you take seriously your church's responsibility to provide for those who serve on church staff (1 Tim. 5:17), then give careful consideration to how you provide for their financial needs. Here are some guidelines that may help with this practical way to meet their needs.

Base salary. One standard for comparison that works well in many communities is to look at what public-school teachers with comparable education and experience earn. Remember, while the school teachers are on a nine- or 10-month contract, your associate staff members will serve your congregation year-round.

Ministry expenses. If the associate staff member will use his or her own car for church business and purchase books and other materials for ministry use, develop a budget for compensation.

Health and life insurance. Be sure your associate staff members have adequate health insurance to address family needs and life insurance to provide for them.

Retirement program. If your denomination or congregation has a retirement plan for your senior pastor, be sure to extend the same benefit to your associate staff members. This benefit will encourage their longevity in ministry.

Vacation time and sabbaticals. Think through your policies on vacation time and extended breaks or sabbaticals for study. Vacation time should be long enough for personal renewal and the opportunity to see extended family. Sabbaticals for study could be part of a package that encourages longevity in ministry. Whatever you do, make it consistent with all your staff.

Continuing education. This topic was discussed above. Be sure that you are providing the opportunity for your associate staff to participate in programs and events that will encourage them and enhance their ministry knowledge and skills.

Tax status. One way you can help your associate staff members is to allow them to pursue licensing or ordination, if that is possible. There is no telling how long the Internal Revenue Service will continue to grant licensed/ordained church workers favorable tax status with regard to housing costs, but as long as there is benefit to your associate staff, give them the opportunity to pursue it if you can.

Allow Flexibility in the Work Schedule

Time demands on people in ministry tend to change with the calendar. When I was on staff, my busiest months were August through October and March through June. When I carried youth-ministry responsibilities, summers were busy as well. There were times during the year when I was out five to six nights a week, and some entire weekends were taken up with retreats or youth trips. When associate staff face busy evenings and weekends, they appreciate being able to take time off without guilt to make up for the extra time they are putting in. In addition, having flexibility to take time out of the office for their own children's school programs, or to be able to do some work at home so they can care for a sick child or spouse, is deeply appreciated. This flexibility reduces the stress they feel in meeting ministry and family needs and helps family members appreciate the church instead of resenting its demands on the staff member.

Build a Personal Support Team

Associate staff members are answerable to their ministry supervisor (generally the senior pastor), and to the committees and boards they report to and work with. While these people can be very supportive, associate staff members may be hesitant to share some struggles and concerns with them. Associate staff can benefit greatly from having a small group of people from the church to meet with regularly whose sole focus is to support them, listen to them, and pray for them. They need a place to be loved and cared for, knowing that whatever they say will remain confidential. If a group like this is to be formed, it should be initiated by the staff member so that he is comfortable with its purpose and those who are a part of it. It may be that he has already addressed this need in other ways.

Respond to Personal and Family Needs

There was a time when I faced a crisis in my family that affected my ability to keep up with the demands of my staff position. There were two boards to which I was answerable, and I shared my problem with the chairs of both boards. Each chair called a special board meeting for me to explain my situation and say which tasks I felt I needed to back off from in my work for the time being. In each case, board members listened to me, affirmed me and my decisions, and prayed for me. In a follow-up, two lay leaders paid a visit to my home, told how God had worked through their own family crises, and prayed with us. While the crisis we faced was difficult, the response of the church to our needs was a tremendous blessing to my family and me. The lay leaders let me know that they cared about me and my family and were willing to pray for me, weep with me, and rejoice with me. Care for your staff and make sure they know that the church will come alongside them in times of need.

5. Other Important Tasks

A few remaining items are important in supporting your associate staff.

Support Your Senior Pastor/Staff Supervisor

The church staff person who directly supervises the associate staff probably has the greatest influence on their longevity and satisfaction in ministry. This person has the challenge of both holding them accountable for their ministry efforts and supporting them in the process, while carrying out her own ministry responsibilities. It is not an easy task! This person will need your encouragement and support as she strives to do this well. Consider occasionally taking some time in your board meetings to focus on this person's work as a ministry supervisor—what's going well, what is a struggle, what help is needed. There may be opportunities for her to attend a course or seminar on supervising associate staff or multiple-staff ministry issues. Look for ways to help your ministry supervisor gain the skills and receive the support needed for this important part of her work. (Appendix A offers suggestions for the supervisor of associate staff members.)

Encourage Commitment and Dependability

One of the greatest pleasures for associate staff is to work with lay volunteers who are committed to their ministry areas and dependable in carrying out their responsibilities. This assistance eliminates many of the headaches of ministry, freeing the staff member to equip and support these people in their ministries. Your board can help by finding ways to reinforce in the congregation the value of the ministries of the church and the importance of people's ministry commitments. You can pursue the development of a churchwide gifts-assessment and ministry-recruitment process that helps people find ministry opportunities that use their gifts and match their priorities and availability. You can encourage ministry groups to have dedication ceremonies for their leaders; regular meetings for support, planning, and skill development; and times of celebration of ministry accomplishments. All of these things help create a climate that encourages commitment and dependability in the volunteers that your associate staff will work with.

Ask How You Can Help

Finally, do not assume that you know what your associate staff people need to thrive in ministry. Take time to ask how they are doing and how their ministries are going. Listen as they share what God is doing and the challenges they face. Ask what you as individuals, and as a board, can do to help them in their ministries. Just to be asked and listened to will mean a lot to them. Whatever they share in answer to your questions, listen carefully and see what steps you can take to support them as they serve your church.

Taking Inventory: Questions for Reflection and Discussion

Some of the questions that follow may be good for you to think about first and then to discuss with others on your board. Some you may want to talk over with the senior pastor, and others you may want to talk about with the church's associate staff members. Each church situation is unique, and these questions may trigger other issues that would be more helpful for you and your board to consider. Use these questions in ways that will be of the most help to you and your church staff.

Creating a Supportive Ministry Environment

1. How is the general "relational health" of our church? What problem areas need our attention as a church board?

2. When was the last time we personally affirmed our associate staff for their ministry gifts and expressed our appreciation to them for the ways they serve our church?

3. Who on our staff tends to function more "behind the scenes" and may benefit from some special encouragement and appreciation?

4. Do the titles we use for our associate staff encourage the kind of respect we would like members of our congregation to have for them?

5. If ordination or licensing is not possible for some of our associate staff,

how else can we promote congregational support for them in their calling to serve the church?

6. Does the congregation see and hear from each of our associate staff often enough to know who they are and to appreciate their contributions to our church?

7. How can we encourage congregation members to express their support and appreciation for our associate staff members?

8. Are we providing the authority and financial resources our associate staff need to carry out their ministries well?

9. Do we as a board have enough times of fellowship with our church staff? Are we getting to know them as people, or do we just know what they do for us?

10. Are we praying regularly for our associate staff members? Are we taking time to find out how we can pray best for them, and are we praying with them as well?

Allowing Associate Staff the Opportunity to Lead

1. Have we clarified with our associate staff members what their job responsibilities are and our expectations of them as staff members? Have we clarified what they can expect from us on the board?

2. How do we tend to respond to new ideas for ministry changes from our associate staff members? Do our responses encourage their initiative and creativity or stifle it? Are we turning them into "ministry maintainers" or allowing them to be ministry leaders?

3. In what ways are we willing to have associate staff members participate on this board?

   a) Do we want them occasionally to bring reports, share their needs, and have us pray for them?

    b) Do we want them present at all or most of our meeting times and to be able to voice their opinions on issues we address?

    c) Do we want them to function as full members of the board, except in those areas where their own work is to be evaluated?

    d) If they do attend portions or all of our meetings where decisions are being made, do we encourage them to share their views?

Providing Associate Staff Opportunities to Grow

1.   Are we providing adequate time and financial support for our associate staff members to pursue continuing-education opportunities? Are we aware of what opportunities they would like to take advantage of if they were able to?

2.   Do we encourage our associate staff to share ministry dreams and goals with us? Do we support them in these pursuits?

3.   Do we have times for reviewing the job descriptions of our associate staff, providing the opportunity for revisions as ministry gifts, needs, and opportunities change?

4.   Are we providing opportunities and financial support for our staff to have group and/or individual retreats for their own spiritual renewal?

5.   When was the last time we had a retreat together with all our staff members, seeking to grow together in Christ? When could we do this again?

Responding to Associate Staff Personal Needs

1.   How do the compensation and benefit packages for our associate staff compare with those of public-school teachers (with similar education and experience) in our community? If this does not seem to be an appropriate comparison, what standard do we want to use?

2.   Have we done a cost-of-living analysis of what it takes to live in our community and provide for families the size of those of our associate staff members?

3. Are we providing adequate ministry expense reimbursement, health and life insurance, retirement plan, vacation time, and continuing-education opportunities for our associate staff?

4. Is there adequate flexibility of work schedule for our staff members to allow them to meet personal and family needs and to balance periods of intense ministry involvement with time off?

5. Do our associate staff members have people in the congregation who function as a support team for them? If not, would they like us to help bring this about?

6. Are we attentive to the personal and family needs of our staff? Do we have the kind of relationship with them that helps us be aware of these kinds of needs, or are we pretty much unaware of their lives outside their work?

Other Items

1. In what ways are we supporting the senior pastor or other supervisor of associate staff in his or her responsibilities? In what ways could we be of more support?

2. In what ways are we encouraging the members of our church to be faithful in their ministries? What else could we do?

3. Have we taken time to sit and listen to our associate staff members and to find out how they would like us to support them in their ministries? If not, when can we do this?

APPENDIX C

The "Thriving in Associate Staff Ministry" Study

Phase I: Focus Group Research

From March 1996 through February 1997, 21 focus groups were conducted in two types of setting. Some were held in the greater Los Angeles area with local long-term associate staff members. Others were held across the United States and Canada in various cities and at national professional association gatherings of associate staff.

Table 1. Types and Locations of Focus Groups

Ministry Group	Number	Description
Children's ministry staff	3	1 at Church Min. Conf., Hume Lake, Calif., 5/96
		2 at Children's Pastors Conference, San Diego, 2/97
Youth ministry staff	3	1 in Los Angeles area, 5/96
		2 at Youth Specialties Conf., Irvine, Calif., 11/96
General Christian ed. staff	3	1 at Church Min. Conf., Hume Lake, Calif., 5/96
		2 at Christian Educators' Conference, Dallas, 1/97
Music/worship staff	3	1 in Los Angeles area, 6/96
		2 at MusiCalifornia Conference, San Diego, 4/96
Women associate staff	3	1 in Los Angeles area, 5/96
		1 at Women's Min. Conf., Pasadena, Calif., 3/96
		1 at Ch. Ministry Conf., Hume Lake, Calif., 5/96
Black church staff	2	1 in Los Angeles area, 2/97
		1 in Dallas, 1/97
Canadian church staff	2	1 in Toronto, Ontario, 6/96
		1 in Calgary, Alberta, 2/97
Associate pastors	1	1 in Dallas, 1/97
Part-time associate staff	1	1 at Church Min. Conf., Hume Lake, Calif., 5/96

The focus groups allow the participants to identify and describe what was helping them thrive in ministry, not just survive. Transcripts were made of focus-group discussions. These were reviewed; the range of issues related to thriving in associate staff ministry was noted. Explanatory comments were analyzed to discern why these issues were important and what contributed to their influence and development. Comparisons were made between groups with similar ministry responsibilities and between different types of groups. The common issues were overwhelming, with few items applicable to only one type of associate staff position. Overall, 73 items were repeated by participants in multiple focus groups, 18 of which related specifically to the supervising pastor. These items were included in the survey developed for phase II of the study.

Phase II: Survey of Long-term Associate Staff

A survey instrument was put together and sent to long-term associate staff members (i.e., with seven years' ministry experience or more) in 14 cooperating denominations across the United States and Canada. The denominations that participated in the survey portion of this study included the following (shown with number of people included and response rates).

Table 2. Denominations Participating in the Survey

Denominations	Number	Responses	Response Rate
U.S. Denominations:			
American Baptist	58	23	40%
Assemblies of God	60	34	57%
Black church staff	71	15	21%
(African Methodist			
Episcopal, Southern			
Baptist, American			
Baptist)			
Christian & Missionary	56	39	70%
Alliance			
Conservative Baptist	63	35	56%
Evangelical Covenant	28	20	71%
Missouri Synod Lutheran	61	24	39%
Presbyterian (U.S.A.)	58	38	66%
Southern Baptist	42	23	55%
United Methodist	65	36	55%

Denominations	Number	Responses	Response Rate
Previous focus group participants	102	67	66%
Canadian Denominations:			
Christian & Missionary Alliance	30	26	87%
Mennonite Brethren	10	7	70%
Pentecostal Assemblies	29	23	79%
United Church of Canada	29	23	79%
Previous focus group participants	13	12	92%
Totals	775	445	57%

The response rates varied greatly from one denomination to another. This discrepancy was due partly to the fact that some denominations had a more difficult time than others in keeping current records on those who serve in associate staff capacities in local churches. Of the 445 responses, 27 were eliminated because the respondent was not thriving in ministry, and four were removed because they had less than the minimum seven years of associate ministry experience. The final result was 414 usable surveys.

Summary of Information About the Survey Participants (n=414)

Gender:	Male: 72%	Female: 28%	
Age:	Mean: 47 years	Range: 27-81 years	
Ethnicity:	Caucasian: 91%	Black: 5%	Other: 4%
Marital status:	Single: 10%	Married: 90%	
Ordination status: (or in process)	Ordained: 66%	Licensed: 20%	Neither: 14%
Member of a professsional association:	Yes: 53%	No: 47%	
Highest degree earned:	High School: 5% M.A./M.Div.: 51%	B.A./B.S.: 31% Doctorate: 7%	Other: 4%
Major(s):	Ministry: 59% Business: 6%	Education (not C.E.): 23% Other: 25%	
Years associate staff:	Mean: 14	Range: 7-51	
No. of churches served:	Mean: 2.7	Range: 1-20	
Years in current church:	Mean: 9	Range: 1-49	
Full-time vs. part-time	Full-time: 84%	Part-time: 16%	
Supervisor:	Sr. pastor: 82%	Other: 18%	
Areas of ministry:	Children: 29% Families: 24% Assoc. Pastor: 36%	Youth: 27% Music: 24% Women's Min.: 9%	Adults: 31% All C.E.: 25% Other: 44%

Country: U.S.A.: 79%   Canada: 21%
Number on staff: Mean: 7   Range: 1-40
Attend church board: Yes: 75%   No: 25%

Factors Identified as Influential for Thriving

Items are listed under the chapters where they are addressed. The percentage score indicates the percent of the respondents who stated that this item was true for them. The mean score indicates the relative influence that the item has on their longevity and satisfaction in ministry. The scale ran from 1 (slightly influential) to 5 (very influential). (n=414)

	%	Mean
Ch. 1: Finding Satisfaction in Following God's Direction		
A sense of fulfillment that comes from using my gifts/abilities in this way.	99%	4.4
A clear sense of calling from God to serve in an associate staff ministry.	92%	4.4
A strong burden, passion, or vision for this kind/type of ministry.	91%	4.3
Ch. 2: Working Well with Your Supervisor and Fellow Associates		
A supportive work relationship with my senior pastor or supervisor.	91%	4.3
Good working relationships with the other associate staff in my church.	86%	4.0
I receive words or notes of appreciation and encouragement from my senior pastor/supervisor.	74%	3.6
As a staff, we enjoy socializing together.	71%	3.4
Our church staff have regular retreats together.	47%	3.3
Ch. 3: Foundational Attitudes and Commitments		
Seeing my kind/type of ministry as "real ministry," not just a stepping stone to something else.	98%	4.6
I strive to remain open to change, learn, grow.	95%	4.2
I am a self-starter in my work and do not need much supervision.	93%	4.2
I am committed to longevity in ministry and strive hard to persevere during difficult times.	93%	4.4
I attend professional conferences, conventions, or other education events for continuing growth and networking with others in my area of ministry.	92%	3.7
I am committed to the success of my senior pastor and seek to find ways to support him/her.	90%	4.1
I strive to keep my focus on the people I serve, not so much on the programs I run.	89%	4.1
I have developed a spirit of contentment in my ministry.	84%	4.0
I have a long-term ministry vision.	79%	4.1
I volunteer for ministry outside of my church (e.g., community, professional, denominational).	76%	3.2
I am involved in mentoring others in ministry.	74%	4.1
I focus my efforts on doing a few things well, and am able to "say no" to other requests.	56%	3.3

Ch. 4: Church Environments that Enable Thriving

	%	Mean
The church lay leadership supports and believes in me.	97%	4.3
Others have affirmed my gifts for ministry.	96%	4.4
The church is very supportive of my area of ministry (i.e., sense of importance, resources).	95%	4.2
I receive words or notes of appreciation and encouragement from those I minister to.	95%	3.6
The church is open to new ideas, new ways of doing ministry (i.e., room for creativity).	93%	4.0
Flexibility to my work schedule allows me to care for my personal and/or family needs.	91%	4.0
Lay staff I work with are committed/dependable.	91%	4.0
My job allows me to have input and to exercise some leadership in the broader church ministry.	91%	4.0
The church provides me with adequate pay and benefits to provide for myself/my family.	90%	3.7
The church I serve is healthy and growing.	88%	4.1
The church provides me with opportunities to pursue continuing education.	84%	3.5
My job description is dynamic, with room for variety and change over time.	83%	3.9
My job is fairly focused, allowing me to concentrate on one area of ministry that I love.	59%	3.7
I delegate a lot of ministry responsibilities to others focusing my efforts in a few areas.	59%	3.5
When I have interviewed at churches, I am very careful and thorough in checking out the pastor, the church, and the job.	52%	4.1

Ch. 5: Sustaining Personal Spiritual Vitality

In my work, I seek God first, and strive to be open to [God's] work in my life and through my life.	93%	4.3
Regular times for prayer.	85%	4.0
I invest time regularly in studying the Bible for my own spiritual growth, not just for my ministry.	82%	3.9
I experience great intimacy with God in worship.	81%	4.0
Besides personal prayer and Bible study, and corporate worship, I have other spiritual disciplines that are an important part of my walk with God.	61%	3.9
I sometimes take extended times away in prayer, like a retreat or partial-day retreat.	48%	3.4

Ch. 6: Building Supportive Relationships

Friendships with members of the congregations.	93%	3.9
Close supportive relationships with selected lay leaders or other members of the congregation.	84%	4.0
Friendships with people outside my church.	76%	3.3
Family members (other than spouse) who support me.	74%	4.0
Regular participation in an accountability or support group of peers in ministry.	58%	3.6
Prayer partner(s) who support me.	58%	3.0
A mentor to whom I can turn for counsel, or who serves as a model for me.	51%	3.7
I belong to a professional organization that focuses on my area of ministry.	47%	3.4

Ch. 7: Strengthening the Home Front   % Mean
A spouse who supports me in my ministry.   87% 4.6
I have been able to maintain a balance in my work and personal life
(e.g., time for fun, family).   82% 3.7

Ch. 8: Savoring Joys and Weathering Storms
I see positive results of my ministry in the lives of those I minister to
(lay leaders, participants).   97% 4.3
I have learned how to handle tough times, to deal with discouragement,
criticism, and difficult people.   91% 3.8

Appendix A: The Valued Supervisor
Let me do my work without "looking over my shoulder" all the time.   93% 4.5
Demonstrate trust in me, his/her belief in my ministry abilities.   92% 4.4
Treat me as a partner in ministry, part of the ministerial team, not just an
assistant.   89% 4.5
Maintain an "open-door" policy, being available when I need to discuss
something with him/her.   89% 4.3
Hold regular (weekly or so) staff meetings.   87% 4.0
Stand by me when I receive criticism.   86% 4.3
Demonstrate loyalty to me as a ministry colleague. 86% 4.3
Communicate his/her appreciation for my ministry efforts.   85% 4.0
Not be threatened by my success in ministry.   84% 4.1
Exhibit stability in his or her own ministry.   83% 4.2
Demonstrate care about me and love for me as a person, not just for
what I do.   82% 4.0
Encourage me to keep learning and growing personally and
professionally.   80% 3.9
Demonstrate genuine interest in my area(s) of ministry.   79% 4.0
Communicate his/her ministry vision and philosophy for the church and
help me understand how what I do contributes to it.   74% 3.9
Encourage and affirm me when I am discouraged.   73% 3.9
Encourage my own spiritual growth and well-being. 73% 3.9

(See also items listed under chapter 2.)

Appendix B: The Supportive Church Board

(See items listed under chapter 4.)

Professional Organizations for Associate Staff Members

One of the keys to thriving in associate staff ministry is the development of supportive relationships with others familiar with the demands of your ministry responsibilities. Across North America, a large number of organizations sponsor conventions, conferences, and seminars where you can connect with others involved in your ministry area. Several groups maintain Web sites with information about training events, helpful resources, and chat rooms where you can talk with other associate staff members. Locally, many cities and states have associations for associate staff based on common ministry responsibilities (e.g., youth pastors, children's ministers, music ministers). It is important that you take the initiative to learn what is available and to connect with others in a mutually supportive fashion. Here are some suggestions for finding organizations that may be of help to you.

Denominational Groups

Be sure to make contact with your denominational leaders to see what kinds of networking groups and support organizations are active within your denomination for people involved in your kind of ministry. You may be surprised to learn that a group already exists, or you may discover others who desire to begin such a group. You could be a catalyst to help organize a group.

Community/Regional Groups

Many communities have ministerial fellowship groups. Some also have groups for those who focus their ministry efforts in a particular area, such as children's ministry, youth ministry, or worship. Check with church staff members in your area to see if they know of any groups that could be of benefit to you. If not, you may find a few people who would like to get together once a month for fellowship, troubleshooting, sharing of resource ideas, prayer, and maybe even some common ministry efforts. Again, you may be a catalyst to a group's formation.

National Organizations

There are a number of ways to locate national groups focused in your ministry area.

1. Ask others you know who have the same kind of ministry focus you do, especially those who have more years of experience.

2. Check magazines or journals devoted to your ministry area. If you are not familiar with any, talk with others in your ministry area. A number of journals today address the needs of different ministry specialties.

3. Search the Internet for Web sites and chat rooms devoted to your ministry area. For associate staff involved in children's or youth ministry, here are a few places to begin:

   Children's Christian Ministries Association:
       www.ccmanetwork.com
   Children's Pastors' Network:
       www.childrensministry.org
   International Network of Children's Ministry:
       www.incm.org
   Group:
       www.grouppublishing.com
   National Network of Youth Ministries:
       www.youthworkers.net

SonLife:
   www.sonlife.com
YouthPastor.com:
   www.youthpastor.com
Youth Specialties:
   www.youthspecialties.com

FURTHER READING FOR ASSOCIATE STAFF MEMBERS

Nuechterlein, Anne Marie. *Improving Your Multiple Staff Ministry: How to Work Together More Effectively*. Minneapolis: Augsburg, 1989.

Nuechterlein, Anne Marie, and Celia Alllison Hahn. *The Male-Female Church Staff*. Bethesda: Alban Institute, 1990.

Oswald, Roy M. *Clergy Self-Care: Finding a Balance for Effective Ministry*. Bethesda: Alban Institute, 1991.

———. *How to Build a Support System for Your Ministry*. Bethesda: Alban Institute, 1991.

Radcliffe, Robert J. *Effective Ministry as an Associate Pastor: Making Beautiful Music as a Ministry Team*. Grand Rapids: Kregel, 1998.

Westing, Harold J. *Multiple Church Staff Handbook* (revised edition). Grand Rapids: Kregel, 1998.